The Man who Drowned the Meadows:

Rowland Vaughan, 1558-1627

The Man who Drowned the Meadows:

Rowland Vaughan, 1558-1627

The Golden Valley Study Group

Logaston Press

LOGASTON PRESS
Little Logaston Woonton Almeley
Herefordshire HR3 6QH
logastonpress.co.uk

First published by Logaston Press 2016
Copyright © Golden Valley Study Group 2016

ISBN 978 1 910839 00 3

Typeset by Logaston Press
and printed and bound in Poland by
www.lfbookservices.co.uk

Front cover: *The Commonwealth from His Booke, see pages 60-61*

CONTENTS

ABBREVIATIONS

The following have been used throughout the book:

AgHR:	Agricultural History Review
HARC:	Herefordshire Archive and Records Centre
HER:	Historic Environment Record, Herefordshire County Council
His Booke:	"Most Approved and Long experienced Water Workes", by Rowland Vaughan, 1610, republished and prefaced by Ellen Beatrice Wood, ed., 1897
LIDAR:	laser-based remote sensing technology
NLW:	National Library of Wales, Aberystwyth
RCHME:	Royal Commission on the Historical Monuments of England
Rowland [unqualified]:	Rowland Vaughan, 1558-1627
TNA:	The National Archives, Kew.
Trans WNFC:	Transactions of the Woolhope Naturalists' Field Club, Hereford

List of Maps, Pedigrees and Figures

PREFACE AND ACKNOWLEDGEMENTS

The concept for this book emerged nearly 20 years ago when a local resident in the Slough valley of west Herefordshire acquired a copy of a dissertation submitted by Penelope Wood to Reading University where she had been studying in the early 1940s. Penelope Bletchly (née Wood) was a daughter of the 19th- and 20th-century owners of the Whitehouse estate, Vowchurch. The subject of the dissertation was the waterworks established by Rowland Vaughan at the Whitehouse in the early 17th century. In fact Rowland's schemes had started earlier at Newcourt, further down the Golden Valley. Rowland, who acquired the Whitehouse estate through marriage, was a man of ideas who published a book in 1610 setting out proposals for social reform, and for improvement of meadow lands by water management schemes.

There was sufficient interest in his schemes for his book to be reprinted in 1897, while in 1936 Gavin Robinson presented a paper to Herefordshire's Woolhope Naturalists' Field Club in which he described the extensive visible evidence remaining of the waterworks schemes in the Golden Valley. The recent rediscovery of Penelope Wood's 1943 study attracted interest locally – we are grateful to the Wood family for supplying a copy of her dissertation and map – and the 'Golden Valley Study Group' (GVSG) came into being to explore local history and topography, and to find out more about Rowland and his works. The members of the Group have enthusiastically researched the subject through fieldwork and archival research and this book is the product of their work.

From 2000 onwards, the GVSG undertook a series of field surveys led by Carl Davies, Martin Kibblewhite and Peter Gunn-Wilkinson which also involved other members of the group. They received useful advice from Keith Ray, county archaeologist. In 2013 the Environment Agency released its Digital Terrain Models (DTM) of river catchments used for flood defence modelling derived from airborne laser scans known as LIDAR (Light Detection and Range). Because of their fine height resolution (less than 10cm) LIDAR-derived DTMs record subtle undulations in ground surface and with appropriate software can reveal earthwork features especially in permanent grassland. David Lovelace collaborated with us in supplying geo-referenced images of landform features throughout the project area.

Some members of the team (in particular Sue Hubbard, Brian Smith, Ruth Richardson and Cynthia Comyn) have spent many hours applying their expertise to recovering and interpreting a hitherto unrecognised wealth of archival sources referring to Rowland's life and family.

External sources of photographs, maps and other illustrations are acknowledged in the text. If not otherwise attributed, the remaining photographs were taken by members of the project team (Carl Davies, Brian Smith, Adrian Holt, Steve Edwards) and are copyright © GVSG.

Keith Taylor kindly piloted the aeroplane that enabled Ian Caves and Adrian Holt to provide us with some fascinating aerial photographs. Steve Edwards was the project co-ordinator.

The members of the project team were: Gill Broadhead, Cynthia Comyn, Carl Davies, Steve Edwards, Peter Gunn-Wilkinson, Adrian Holt, Sue Hubbard, Martin Kibblewhite, Ruth Richardson, Brian Smith and Rosemary Vaughan. It has been a cooperative group project – all have contributed their time and expertise in varying ways, so we have not assigned individual authorship to the chapters or to the book as a whole. We are also grateful to the Executive Committee of the GVSG for its encouragement and financial support and to the Woolhope Naturalists' Field Club for continuing their grant from our previous publication on Turnastone.

This is the second book produced by the Golden Valley Study Group. We especially thank Andy and Karen Johnson and Logaston Press for again agreeing to publish this long-planned work.

Steve Edwards, Editor

One Mile

One Kilometre

RIVER WYE

BREDWARDINE

STRETTON SUGWAS

DORSTONE

HAY ON WYE

WILMASTON

HEREFORD

PETERCHURCH

POSTON

CRASWALL

VOWCHURCH

PORTHAML

TURNASTONE

Golden Valley

ALLENSMORE

WHITE HOUSE

TALGARTH

NEWCOURT

JURY FARM

BACTON

Black Mountains

LONGTOWN

DORE ABBEY

RIVER DORE

PONTRILAS

BRECKNOCK

HEREFORDSHIRE

RIVER MONNOW

RIVER WYE

MONMOUTHSHIRE

LLANROTHAL

ABERGAVENNY

RIVER USK

MONMOUTH

Frontispiece: General map of the area showing the main places referred to in the text.
(Drawn by Mr Geoff Gwatkin)

1 INTRODUCTION

The year was 1610. King James I had been on the throne of England for seven years, yet the excitement and entrepreneurism of the Elizabethan age continued. In that year a 154-page book was published in London by Rowland Vaughan, Esq., with the title: *Most Approved and Long experienced Water Workes.* The subtext read: *Containing the manner of Winter and Summer drowning of Medow and Pasture, by the advantage of the least, River, Brooke, Found, or Water-prill adjacent; there-by to make those grounds (especially if they be drye) more Fertile Ten for One. As also a demonstration of a Project, for the great benefit of the Common-wealth generally, but of Hereford-shire especially.*[1]

The setting for Vaughan's book is the Golden Valley of south-west Herefordshire, close to the Welsh border, which he describes as 'the Paradise of al the parts beyond the Severn', ... 'the Lombardy of Herefordshire, the Garden of the Old Gallants and Paradice of the backside of the Principallitie'.[2] Many who live in or visit the area today would not disagree with such a description. Original copies of the 1610 edition are very rare and difficult to find; indeed it might have receded into obscurity but for a 19th-century editor, Ellen Beatrice Wood of Hertford, who arranged for it to be reprinted in 1897, retaining the original spelling and punctuation but with modernised typography. The Wood edition is now easily accessible in facsimile, either online or through 'print to order' booksellers. Although the word 'book(e)' does not appear in Vaughan's original title, Wood's version was titled *Rowland Vaughan, his Booke. Published 1610.* For convenience hereafter we shall refer to the work as *His Booke*, and to its author as 'Rowland'. Spelling of the name varies in different sources, but we shall maintain consistency. Others with the same name will be differentiated by suitable qualifiers (*e.g.* Rowland Vaughan of Porthaml).

The Herefordshire Golden Valley takes its name from the river Dore, which arises in the uplands around Merbach Hill to the west of Hereford and proceeds in a south-easterly direction down the gently sloping valley to its confluence with the Monnow below Pontrilas. There are various suggestions[3] for the origin of the name, but the most plausible is a misinterpretation of the Welsh word '*dwr*' meaning 'water'. The names of many southern English rivers from the Thames westwards have retained their pre-Saxon (*i.e.* Celtic or ancient British) names and Welsh influence and language were strong in this area until relatively recent centuries, as seen in the many Welsh-derived place names. The medieval Cistercian abbey was named Dore, from the river. It appears that 16th-century antiquarians misinterpreted this as '*d'or*' or golden, leading the cartographer Christopher Saxton in 1577 to refer to 'the gilden vale'.

The use of surnames came late to Wales and many transitional forms are encountered in the 16th and 17th centuries. Evidence of the traditional patronymic system is seen in the use of ap Harry (son of Harry) which subsequently became fixed and anglicised as Parry (a family that we shall meet later). The surname Vaughan is common in the Welsh borders, which makes genealogical research difficult, and has its origin in the Welsh word *bychan*, meaning 'small' or 'little one'. After a personal name, this would mutate to *fychan* used in the sense of 'the younger' in English, typically to distinguish fathers and sons with the same personal name. Single 'f' in Welsh is pronounced as English 'v' and thus *fychan* became anglicised as Vaughan, and the aspirated 'gh' became silent.[4]

The flat meadow lands of the valley bottom were ideal for controlled flooding, or 'drowning', to improve their fertility, whether by the monks of Dore Abbey or, later, by Rowland Vaughan, a work he began in the 1580s after his first marriage and the consequent acquisition of Newcourt at Bacton. We shall explore his own account of the waterworks in *His Booke*, attempting to assess the long term impact, if any, in the Golden Valley and also on agricultural practices in other parts of the country. We shall also see how other aspects of his turbulent life such as lengthy and complex lawsuits, as well as severe financial problems, impeded progress with his ambitious ideas.

By Rowland's time the Golden Valley was an area of gentry landowners, with relatively small manorial estates. In 1545 the largest tax-payers (over ten shillings) in the area included (among others) Thomas Berowe, George ap Harry (Turnastone/Poston), Roger Vaughan (Bacton), John Baskerville, Simon ap Harry (Chanstone/Walterstone), Richard Delahay, and Sir Richard Vaughan (Bredwardine), names that we shall meet again in our story.[5]

Rowland was himself born into a landed gentry family with extensive holdings in Brecknockshire and Herefordshire. He was the son of Watkyn Vaughan of Bredwardine and grandson of Sir William Vaughan of Porthaml. His mother Joan was of the Parry family and he used this connection through his great-aunt, Blanche Parry, Chief Gentlewoman of Queen Elizabeth's Privy Chamber, to gain an introduction to the court of Queen Elizabeth I. This was not a success and he was eventually packed off for several unhappy and unhealthy years of military service in Ireland. As described in *His Booke* he returned to his father's house in Herefordshire 'for recovery of my health which within six months I obteined'.[6]

His Booke has a polemical but discursive, meandering style making it difficult to follow the arguments propounded; at intervals Rowland digresses to launch a diatribe against some cause or person. In the interests of clarity we have used verbatim quotations sparingly, but have paraphrased and condensed the main elements. In this introductory chapter we provide an outline of the main topics that *His Booke* addresses. In subsequent chapters we provide more detailed information about Rowland's complex life story and his family, so far as can be determined from archival research. We describe his proposals for social reform, and discuss in some detail the nature and extent of his water management scheme, which together form the core of *His Booke*. Using traditional and modern digital survey and mapping techniques we investigate the field evidence of his water-works, still visible today, and attempt to put them in context of other 17th-century schemes in the Marches and in the south of England.

Rowland's marriage in 1582 to his cousin Elizabeth Vaughan brought him to Newcourt at Bacton in the Golden Valley. This gave him the opportunity to start implementing his ideas for water management in the meadows, as well as exploiting the power of water through water mills. Although he claims in *His Booke* to be a pioneer of these techniques, it is known that similar schemes were being developed elsewhere, and he mentions other landowners who had expressed an interest. It is known that Cistercian monks actively deployed the principles of water management in support of their farming enterprises, notably at Buildwas in Shropshire, although the evidence for Dore Abbey is limited to landscape features revealed by LIDAR. Certainly Rowland appears to be the first to commit the concepts and principles to print.

Also at Newcourt Rowland started developing his ideas for social reform, which form a large part of the first half of *His Booke*. Introducing a proposed 'common-wealth' he commented that within 1½ miles of his house were 500 poor dwellings.[7] This was undoubtedly an exaggeration; for example the hearth tax returns for 1664 show a total of 184 houses for the combined parishes of Bacton, Vowchurch, Turnastone and Peterchurch.[8] Nevertheless, he used it to justify his plan to build a mill at the centre of a working community of 2000 'mechanicals'[9] encompassing a list of over 40 skills or trades. All would have equal status, with no hierarchy. Accommodation and food would be provided for all. There is no evidence this scheme was ever realised, probably through lack of financial backing, but a rather fanciful illustration from *His Booke* shows a schematic of how he envisaged it operating (see cover, and Fig. 5.3).

Although not the main focus of *His Booke,* Rowland takes time out from page 50 onwards to air another of his passions, the weirs on the River Wye, complaining at length that the Commissioners of Weirs acting through vested interests were working against the livelihoods of the local people. By removing the weirs, the river would become navigable and we could 'have wine with our venison' (whereas, as he complained, overland carriage from London 'makes a cup of claret look like a weak lean wench that hath the green sickness').[10]

As a Wye Commissioner, Rowland would have been aware of the developing iron industry in the lower reaches of the Wye around Tintern, with new blast furnaces and forges replacing traditional technologies deployed in the Forest of Dean. The Golden Valley lacked a source of iron ore, but what it had in abundance was timber. Seizing a chance in 1593 by paying off debts for his cousin James Parry of Poston, Rowland acquired the timber rights to Snodhill Park. This enabled him, with business partners, and again exploiting water power, to set up a forge (and possibly a sawmill) at Peterchurch which survived into the 18th century.

Another of Rowland's interests was the Church. He declared himself 'no papist, nor puritan, but a true protestant according to the king's injunctions'.[11] He was concerned about the lingering seeds of Catholicism fostered by former monks from Dore Abbey, while he lamented the lack of preaching in the Golden Valley. At various times he was patron for the parishes of Bacton, Peterchurch, Turnastone and Vowchurch, which led to his involvement in appointments of clergy. However, he failed in his duties to maintain the fabric of the buildings and churchyards, because he could not afford it.

Rowland's first wife Elizabeth died *c.*1588 but he had the legal right to continue occupying Newcourt for his lifetime. Some time afterwards (*c.*1593-95) he remarried to Anne Jones, who again brought him a property, Whitehouse on the borders of Vowchurch, Turnastone and St Margaret's parishes. Anne's death date is not known, but once again he inherited the lifetime occupancy of the house. His third marriage, to Elizabeth Prosser, happened between 1611 and 1613 and around that time he started to declare himself 'of Whitehouse'. The eventual heir of Whitehouse after Rowland died would be Anne's younger sister and through her, her husband Epiphan Howorth. Howorth initially tried to help Rowland manage his finances, but his continuing inability to pay his debts eventually threatened his interest in Whitehouse and led to Howorth's successful legal claim to Whitehouse whilst Rowland was still alive, and he and his family were evicted in 1625. He died in 1627 and his only memorials (apart from *His Booke*) are a mention on his third wife's monument in Peterchurch, and a small shield displaying his arms in the nave at Vowchurch.

So we come to the main business, Rowland's 'Most approved and long-experienced water-workes'. It is obvious to anyone walking the meadows and footpaths in the Peterchurch and Turnastone area that various man-made ditches and channels exist. Further, there is undocu-mented local awareness, probably maintained through generations of oral tradition, that these irrigation schemes date back several centuries. Despite later disruptions, including the building of the Golden Valley railway in the 1870s and changing agricultural practices, it was still possible in the 20th century to find evidence of Rowland's waterworks, as was noted by Gavin Robinson in 1936.[12] A detailed description is provided in a student dissertation, dated 1943, by Penelope Wood of Whitehouse, a descendant of Epiphan Howorth.[13] It appears, from her maps and descriptions informed by her family's knowledge dating back to the early 20th century, that more of Rowland's work was visible on the ground 70 years ago than can be traced today. The next major survey, from 1982 to 1983, was a government-funded scheme under the Manpower Services Commission, led by Rosamund Skelton, which made a detailed field and hedgerow study, together with an archaeological survey in the Peterchurch area. Although not formally published, the reports, including a chapter on water management, are available in the Historic Environment Record (HER) in Herefordshire Archives and Record Centre. In 2004, English Heritage conducted a detailed survey of post-medieval water systems at Turnastone Court farm, including the visible remains of Rowland's waterworks. All of these studies, together with our own extensive results from field walking and observation, ground-based and aerial photog-raphy, and application of digital mapping and LIDAR surveys, have been incorporated into our own studies of the waterworks. This has enabled us to present a comprehensive view of how Rowland's system may have worked, what of it can still be traced today, and what has been its wider impact on water meadow management techniques.

2 THE VAUGHAN FAMILY

Rowland Vaughan was born in 1558 or 1559, the second son of Watkyn Vaughan of Bredwardine and Moccas and his wife Joan, and he died in 1627 at the then advanced age of 69. No portrait of him is known but his apparel may be imagined from the contemporary monument to the Smalman family in Kinnersley church (Fig. 2.1).[1] His birthplace, like his exact date of birth, is uncertain but it was probably in a house built in the ruins of Bredwardine Castle. The first of the family recorded at Bredwardine was Walter Seys (derived from the Welsh *sais* for Englishman or English-speaking) in the reign of Edward III (1312-77) but the first to have the surname Vaughan was Sir Roger Vaughan[2] of Bredwardine, who died at Agincourt in 1415. His monument in Bredwardine church (Fig. 2.2) would have been very familiar to Rowland. The Vaughan demesne included the adjacent Norman church of St Andrew, lengthened, redecorated and with a chancel rebuilt in about 1300. Here Rowland, shortly after his birth, would have been baptised in the massive Norman font (Fig. 2.3). In the 12th century the old castle had boasted a garden, kitchen garden, orchard, fish ponds, vineyard and a park.[3] Although abandoned when the Vaughans acquired the castle and grounds in the later medieval period, it is likely that fruit and plants gone wild still grew here. It would have been an idyllic children's playground, especially as the whole demesne overlooked the River Wye.

We do not have any details of Rowland's childhood years, but he and his siblings may have begun learning their letters from their mother Joan.

Fig. 2.1 The Smalman family monument in Kinnersley (1633) showing clothing characteristic of the period.

Fig. 2.2 Monument to
Sir Roger Vaughan at
Bredwardine, who died at
Agincourt, 1415.

Fig. 2.3 The Norman font
in Bredwardine church,
where Rowland would have
been baptised.

At age 5, the boys would have commenced a more formal study programme including reading and some writing in English, simple arithmetic, and basic Latin. Watkyn may have engaged a tutor for them but that was expensive, so it is possible that their teacher was the parish priest. Indeed, Rowland's later style in *His Booke*[4] owed a great deal to his learning to write in 'Bible' English.[5] His older brother Henry would inherit the estate and so needed to understand management, but Rowland would have to make his fortune in other ways. His activities in later life show that he was not studious, rarely settled long at anything and relished being argumentative. Both boys, though, enjoyed their lessons in horsemanship and weaponry. At about 7 years old, following the common pattern for gentry boys, they should have transferred to a grammar school, probably at Hereford or Brecon. Here the main teaching would be Latin and possibly Greek. At about 14, boys usually progressed to university, where philosophy and some maths were added, before completing their education by studying law. However, Rowland in *His Booke* described his education, and lack of knowledge of literature, as that of a soldier,[6] so if he did receive any higher education he may not have been an attentive scholar. He would later enter his own eldest son for Jesus College, Oxford and the Inner Temple, which suggests Rowland's perceived rise in society. That Henry's and Rowland's names do not appear in the relevant registers for either Oxford, Cambridge or the four Inns of Court may indicate that their father simply could not afford the necessary fees.

The Vaughan house has gone but the demesne probably included the 14th-century manor house of Old Court (Fig. 2.4), now a farmhouse, which retains traces of painted flowers and the upper part of, perhaps, an angel on the wood of the through passage. Both this house and Bredwardine church retain much of the carving and medieval stonework that Rowland knew,

Fig. 2.4 Old Court, Bredwardine, with parts dating from the 14th century.
(Drawing copied courtesy of Richard and Brenda Stokes)

Fig. 2.5 Medieval stained glass in St Michael's church, Moccas.
Rowland would almost certainly have known these windows. The figures give an idea of the type of
clothing worn at the time by working men.

but it is at St Michael's church, Moccas that some of the evocative colour that transformed
these buildings can be seen most clearly. This lovely Norman church still has parts of two
beautiful 14th-century stained-glass windows (Fig. 2.5).[7] A small castle site to the south-west
of the church may have had an early small deer park attached.[8] Most of the present Moccas
park is in Dorstone parish and there is evidence for it in 1317,[9] but the deer park is not shown
on Christopher Saxton's 1577 map of Herefordshire. Lord Burghley – Queen Elizabeth's Lord
Treasurer, and the most powerful minister in her government – annotated his own copy to
show both Bredwardine and Moccas as the property of Watkyn Vaughan (Map 2.1).[10] However
it is possible that Watkyn Vaughan could not afford the upkeep of such a prestigious park and
it had fallen into a state of neglect. Nevertheless, this whole area was home to the Vaughan children and Henry as an adult would live in the manor in Moccas. In due course, Henry's eldest
son, Rowland's nephew, would return the focus of the estate to Bredwardine when he repaired,
or rebuilt, the house among the remains of the castle in *c*.1639-40.

The Vaughan family had attempted to raise their status by acquiring an English surname.
Indeed, a stranger riding through the Welsh March four or five hundred years ago might reasonably have believed that every passing castle and mansion in the countryside belonged to the
same family of Vaughan. Apart from Bredwardine and Moccas, in the 50 miles from Kington to
Abergavenny there were related Vaughans in Huntington and Hergest, and on the Welsh side of
the border there were Vaughans with further wide estates between Brecon and Hay-on-Wye, at
Tretower and Porthaml. All were Anglo-Welsh Tudor supporters, rewarded by Tudor monarchs
with former monastic lands and with public office in Brecon and Herefordshire. However,
not all Vaughans were related. The name was an English version of Welsh *fychan*, meaning
the 'small' or 'youngest' one in any family (see Chapter 1). Welsh gentry families were early to
adopt the English style of surname, most changing from the patronymic tradition of using *ap*
(son of) so that Howell ap Harri (son of Harri) became Howell Parry, and ap Howell became
Powell. From about 1400 the descendants of the various *fychans* started to use this as a surname

Map 2.1 Saxton's map of Herefordshire, 1577. Detail of the Dore and Wye valleys
showing handwritten annotations including Watkyn Vaughan (Bredwardine/Moccas),
Parry (Poston), ap Harry (Morehampton) and Vaughan (Newcourt).
(© The British Library Board, Royal 18 D.III f.95)

Fig. 2.6 Signatures of Rowland Vaughan and his son John on a sealed document in the Herefordshire Archive and Records Centre (HARC).
(HARC AW28/25/9; thanks to Rhys Griffith for photography)

in the English manner. The anglicised spelling was not at first standardised and even in 1600 it was still pronounced in the Golden Valley as Vahens, Vahan, Vahoan and Vahaen, with an aspirated 'h' derived from Welsh 'ch'. Lord Burghley wrote Vaughn but Rowland signed himself as Vaughan (Fig. 2.6). He was proud of his Welsh ancestry, drawing attention in *His Booke* to the line of his forefathers.[11]

Confusingly, Watkyn Vaughan, Rowland's father, occasionally had his first name anglicised to Walter. He would later be described as 'a good honest gentleman' in a letter written by William Cecil, a cousin of Lord Burghley, who lived in the Cecils' ancestral family home of Allt-yr-Ynys, in nearby Walterstone.[12] Watkyn was himself a second son of Sir William Vaughan of Porthaml, near Talgarth. He needed to better himself in society in order to raise the prospects for his immediate family. Two of the accepted routes to achieving this were to hold public office and to acquire patronage, the latter more secure if it involved a family member. Patronage and family connections were the recognised and indisputable routes for advancement in the hierarchical Tudor society. If you could attach yourself to someone of a higher social status then you could lay claim to being sponsored by them. Being a relative not only carried additional cachet but also made it more likely that the appeal for sponsorship would be successful. It is clear that Sir William Vaughan fully realised the potential for his son, and his grandson, because he allied them both to the Parry (ap Harry) family, whose most influential member was Blanche, the Chief Gentlewoman of Queen Elizabeth I's Privy Chamber and the close confidante of the queen herself.

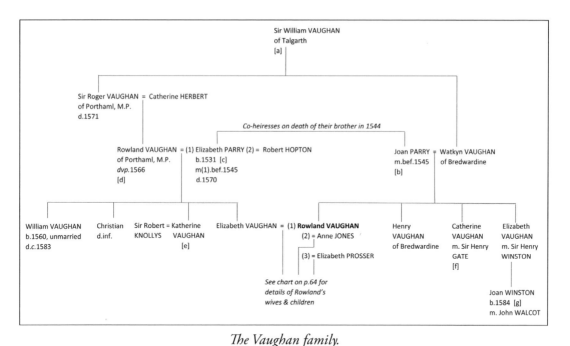

```
                              Sir William VAUGHAN
                              of Talgarth
                              [a]


    Sir Roger VAUGHAN = Catherine HERBERT
    of Porthaml, M.P.
    d.1571
                              Co-heiresses on death of their brother in 1544

    Rowland VAUGHAN = (1) Elizabeth PARRY (2) = Robert HOPTON        Joan PARRY = Watkyn VAUGHAN
    of Porthaml, M.P.      b.1531 [c]                                m.bef.1545   of Bredwardine
    dvp.1566              m(1).bef.1545                              [b]
    [d]                   d.1570


William VAUGHAN  Christian  Sir Robert = Katherine   Elizabeth VAUGHAN = (1) Rowland VAUGHAN   Henry      Catherine    Elizabeth
b.1560, unmarried  d.inf.   KNOLLYS    VAUGHAN                        (2) = Anne JONES        VAUGHAN    VAUGHAN      VAUGHAN
d.c.1583                               [e]                                                   of Bredwardine  m. Sir Henry  m. Sir Henry
                                                       (3) = Elizabeth PROSSER                           GATE         WINSTON
                                                                                                         [f]
                                              See chart on p.64 for
                                              details of Rowland's                                                 Joan WINSTON
                                              wives & children                                                     b.1584 [g]
                                                                                                                   m. John WALCOT
```

The Vaughan family.
(a) guardian of Joan & Elizabeth Parry (b) age 13y 7m in 1544 (c) age 12 on 26 Jun 1543
(d) M.P. for Co. Brecon; sometime Groom of the Chamber to Elizabeth I
(e) named in Blanche Parry's will 1589 (f) m. by 1584; Sir Henry d. after 1589
(g) Rowland's 'Welsh Niece'

Marriage amongst the gentry class was a matter of social advancement and business. If the two young people fell in love then that was an added bonus for them but rarely the reason for a marriage which had been arranged by their parents. Watkyn was married to Joan, daughter of Blanche Parry's brother Milo ap Harry[13] and Eleanor Scudamore. Watkyn's father had, therefore, joined their family to families with royal court connections and of sufficient note also to include men in public office. In fact, the connections were considered so advantageous that two marriages were arranged: Watkyn with Joan, and Joan's sister Elizabeth with Watkyn's nephew, Rowland Vaughan of Porthaml. The latter (who would become a Member of Parliament) was the son of Watkyn Vaughan's older brother, Roger. At the time neither sister was expected to inherit the Parry estates as they had an older brother, Henry, but he died in 1544 and the sisters became co-heiresses.[14]

The sisters' marriage arrangements were actually facilitated by their brother's death. At the time wardship of minors was common.[15] If the male heir to an estate was a minor (under 21 years) when his father died then the boy would become a ward of the Crown. The king could then give, or more usually sell, the wardship. The person buying this agreed to manage the estate during the minority and hand the estate over to the heir in good order when the ward came of age. It also meant that the buyer could control the business arrangement of the heir's marriage. The heir would be the eldest surviving son but if only daughters survived then they were joint, or co-heiresses. Milo ap Harry died in 1543 and his son in 1544. This left the two girls, Joan and Elizabeth, as heiresses to both their father and brother. Sir William Vaughan

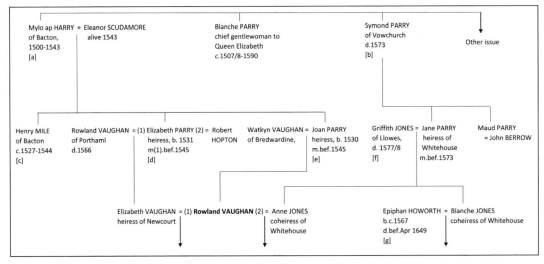

Mylo ap HARRY = Eleanor SCUDAMORE	Blanche PARRY	Symond PARRY

Mylo ap HARRY = Eleanor SCUDAMORE
of Bacton, alive 1543
1500-1543
[a]

Blanche PARRY
chief gentlewoman to
Queen Elizabeth
c.1507/8-1590

Symond PARRY
of Vowchurch
d.1573
[b]

Other issue

Henry MILE
of Bacton
c.1527-1544
[c]

Rowland VAUGHAN = (1) Elizabeth PARRY (2) = Robert
of Porthaml   heiress, b. 1531   HOPTON
d.1566   m(1).bef.1545
                 [d]

Watkyn VAUGHAN = Joan PARRY
of Bredwardine,   heiress, b. 1530
                  m.bef.1545
                  [e]

Griffith JONES = Jane PARRY
of Llowes,   heiress of
d. 1577/8   Whitehouse
                  m.bef.1573
[f]

Maud PARRY
= John BERROW

Elizabeth VAUGHAN = (1) Rowland VAUGHAN (2) = Anne JONES
heiress of Newcourt   coheiress of
                                               Whitehouse

Epiphan HOWORTH = Blanche JONES
b.c.1567   coheiress of Whitehouse
d.bef.Apr 1649
[g]

Rowland's Parry relatives.
(a) heir to his father aged 24 in 1524; d. 12 Jan 1543; IPMs 5 Aug 1543, 31 Oct 1545
(b) lord of Bacton, owner of Whitehouse; will dated 23 Jun 1573; proved PCC 13 Jul 1573
(c) Age 16+ in 1543, unmarried, d. 27 Feb 1644; IPM 16 May 1644. His surname is obviously an Anglicised form of patronymic, from his father Milo
(d) age 12 on 26 Jun 1543, one of the heiresses of her brother
(e) age 13y 7m in 1544, one of the heiresses of her brother
(f) also of Whitehouse jure uxoris, will dated 19 Aug 1577, proved PCC 28 Jun 1578
(g) of Whitehouse jure uxoris, will dated 7 Oct 1643, proved PCC 28 Apr 1649

of Talgarth astutely bought their wardships and so had the right to arrange their marriages. Although this sounds strange now, at the time it was accepted procedure and it is probable that the girls knew their prospective husbands well. By November 1545 Sir William had married Joan, about 15 years old, to his second son Watkyn Vaughan, and 14 year old Elizabeth to his grandson Rowland Vaughan of Porthaml.

Watkyn and Joan, now living at Bredwardine, began a family of their own which included Henry, their two daughters Catherine and Elizabeth, and the impetuous Rowland. Watkyn took his family duties very seriously. He served in public office in Breconshire from 1551 until the 1590s when age and infirmity meant that he asked to be relieved of the Deputy Lieutenancy in favour of his son Henry.[16] He also held public office in Herefordshire from 1552, serving as a Justice of the Peace c.1574-96 and in this capacity submitted bills to be considered by Parliament.[17] These bills he sent to Blanche Parry, Joan's aunt, for the queen's perusal. He made the most of this family connection and, through Blanche, with her cousin Lord Burghley. Indeed, Watkyn maintained a regular correspondence with Blanche. In a long letter sent by him to Lord Burghley on 17 December 1584 he mentioned that: 'I have sent instructions for two bills to Mrs [Mistress] Blanche, good my Lord'.[18]

In time, Watkyn used his enhanced position to arrange the future for his own children. Eventually the girls, well trained by Joan in managing a household and servants, would in their turn be married. Elizabeth married Henry Winston, of Standish in Gloucestershire, while

Catherine married, in 1584, as his second wife, Sir Henry Gate, who had connections with the royal court. Watkyn, writing from Bredwardine, took care to apprise Lord Burghley of this family news. His letter provides a fascinating insight into Watkyn's personality as it is partly written in doggerel verse. Clearly he felt he knew Lord Burghley sufficiently well not to have to write formally.[19] Watkyn and Joan were obviously very pleased when their girls were so well settled. Henry would inherit the estate so his future was secure. Rowland though, a second son like his father, would need additional help.[20] It was reasonable that they could hope for sponsorship from his cousin Rowland Vaughan of Porthaml, for it is likely that he was young Rowland's godfather.

This certainly seemed a very reasonable prospect, for Rowland Vaughan, married to Elizabeth, Joan's sister, had prospered. Their home was at Great Porthaml, near Talgarth, where their children, William, Christian (a girl who died young), Katherine and little Elizabeth passed their early childhood. The house is now a modern farm with an impressively grand 16th-century gate tower at its entrance (Fig. 2.7) and internal medieval architectural features.[21] The Porthaml estates stretched up to Dinas and Brecknock Mere (Llangorse Lake) and Bronllys. When the Parry estates were rather unequally partitioned between the sisters, Elizabeth's English part of her inheritance included the Newcourt estate at Bacton in Herefordshire. However, Rowland Vaughan of Porthaml did not just lead the life of a local landowner, for he became MP for Brecon and one of the six Grooms of the Chamber to Queen Elizabeth I. This link with the royal court was clearly facilitated by the family connection with Blanche Parry.

Blanche kept family contact for, although she never returned to Herefordshire, she maintained a close interest in the area of her childhood through her younger brother. She knew the situation in Bacton parish for, years after Rowland the MP's death, Blanche noted in her

Fig. 2.7 The gatehouse at Great Porthaml, Talgarth

first will of 1578 that: 'Where as the vicar of Bacton lacketh a house to inhabit in and that my nephew Roland Vaughan and his wife did grant away the house wherein the vicar was accustomed to dwell; I will and require my Lord Treasurer [Lord Burghley] to take order that William Vaughan at his full age shall make a grant of that house or some other house meet for the purpose to be assured to the vicar and his successors ...'.[22] It may be that Rowland (of Porthaml) and Elizabeth had decided to cease what in effect was a subsidy to the Church, or that they had simply needed money. Blanche's statement is not accusatory even as she attempted to rectify the situation through their son William. Indeed, Blanche favoured William in this, her first will but he predeceased her in 1583.

Rowland Vaughan MP of Porthaml was buried in St Margaret's church, Westminster on 19 January 1566. Blanche arranged his funeral for the queen's accounts record a payment of £20 to 'Mrs. Blaunche Apparie, 28th of January 1565 [that is 1566] for the Funeral of Mr. Vaughan',[23] showing that the queen actually paid these funeral expenses (in today's currency, about £3,400). This was an unusual gesture from the often parsimonious queen and strongly implies a personal royal favour for Blanche. His widow, Elizabeth, made a settlement of her lands for the benefit of herself and her children. When she remarried, her second husband being Robert Hopton, Marshall of the Household at the royal court, these land deeds were handed to Watkyn Vaughan of Bredwardine, her former brother-in-law. When Elizabeth herself died in 1570, the children's nearest relatives were their step-father, and their Uncle Watkyn and Aunt Joan of Bredwardine.

The evidence shows that Watkyn and Joan would later bring up their Winston grandchildren after their mother died. It is a reasonable assumption, due to the land deeds, that they also took their nephew and nieces into their household. It is also possible that Robert Hopton kept contact with his step-children, especially as he had estates in Herefordshire, and was a Justice of the Peace for the shire. He did relinquish his court position in 1577 but, as he continued to live mainly in London until his death in 1590, he could still offer sponsorship. Blanche Parry too could be called upon to help for, after all, Queen Elizabeth had favoured their father through her by paying his funeral expenses. Meanwhile, Watkyn and Joan could be relied upon

Fig. 2.8 Blanche Parry monument at Bacton church,
showing Blanche in attendance on Queen Elizabeth I.

to do their best for the children. They were evidently kind and hospitable, welcoming children related to them to their family home. It was probably in this way that their son Rowland, now about 12 years old, and presumably at grammar school, came to know well his cousins and perhaps especially Elizabeth.

Although it was common practice to provide a home for children within the extended family who had lost a parent, it could still be a drain on resources. It was only natural that Watkyn and Joan would tentatively consider that a particularly advantageous option would be, if it proved possible, to re-unite at least partly the two halves of the estate inherited by Joan and her sister.[24] However, this seemed most unlikely as William had inherited their mother's portion. Therefore, in 1571, their prime concern was what to do with young Rowland. 'London was the place to be if what [you] wanted was to taste the remarkable cultural ferment of the Tudor age',[25] and young Rowland was clearly ambitious. So Watkyn Vaughan contacted Blanche for her help and sponsorship. She immediately arranged to employ him as her attendant. This is made clear in a letter from William Cecil of Allt-yr-Ynys to his cousin Lord Burghley in which he describes Rowland as 'strong and active and attended my good friend Mrs Blanche Parry, his aunt, when he was a youth and if God had pleased, she would have preferred him to a better room, for that he is son to a good honest gentleman'.[26] It was Blanche's death in 1590 and so the diminution of her influence, which stopped Rowland's advancement at the royal court, his own merits apparently being insufficient. That telling phrase 'if God had pleased' highlights his unsuitability. Rowland loved new ideas, often wanting to improve things, but he lacked patience and determination, and perhaps too the ability to dissemble, necessary for success at the royal court.

Rowland himself described this time: 'After I had spent some yeares in Queene Elizabeths Court, and saw the greatnes and glory thereof under the command of Mistress Blanch Parry (an honorable & vertuous gentlewoman, my aunt and mistresse), my spirit beeing too tender to indure the bitternesse of her humor; I was by her carefull (though crabbed) austerity forced unto the Irish Wars.'[27] Blanche, a courtier of great experience, employed Rowland for several years but seems to have found him unable, or unwilling, to work at anything for long, making his advancement difficult. She knew Rowland's limitations and was not charmed by his sulkiness. In his turn, Rowland wanted to widen his horizons but she evidently refused him further financial support. Disappointed, he described her carefulness as 'crabbed' but was, nevertheless, sufficiently fair to acknowledge Blanche's influence. Indeed, Blanche, for her part, seems to have helped him further, for his military service may have been sponsored by Sir John Perrot, who was a friend of Blanche and remembered in her final will of 1589. Blanche's valuable influence can be discerned in that she received official correspondence for the queen from Ireland. Sir John was given responsibilities in Ireland in 1570-73, being appointed Lord President of Munster in 1571. He returned to Ireland as Lord Deputy of Ireland in 1584, his tour of duty only ending in 1588. Blanche helped her great-nephew as much as she could but it was probably a relief for both when their ways parted.

Rowland's service in Ireland occurred between 1575 and 1580. Ireland had long been an area of disaffection. Feudalism prevailed and different clans and groupings often fought each other. In particular southern Ireland, the provinces of Munster and South Leinster, were dominated by the Butler family of Ormonde and the FitzGeralds of Desmond. Adding to the power struggle was the attempt by the Crown, from the 1530s to 1603, to extend English influence and laws. Although local unrest was always prevalent, the most serious fighting started in 1579 when Rowland was in his early 20s. During this Desmond Rebellion, of 1579-83, the troops mustered in 1580 included men from Herefordshire.[28] Rowland described the conditions in Ireland: 'I continued three or foure years some-times twist [waist] deep in that country-water & what with long fasting and ill diet, I was possessed with the country-disease: the extremity wherof hasted mee to returne to my Fathers home in the County of Heref. for recovery of my health which within six months I obteined.'[29] So he returned home, suffering from marsh malaria, or dysentery, which he attributed to the unhealthy bogs of Ireland, combined with poor quality army food.

When Rowland returned from the Irish Wars he lacked a patron as Blanche seems to have been unwilling to help him further; he was not mentioned in her first, nuncupative will of 1578 made when she thought she was dying. Despite this setback, Rowland craved the excitement of the royal court even if he would only be on the periphery of activity. He wrote that 'I remember in Queene Elizabeths days my Lady of Warwick, Mistresse Blanch Parry and my Lady Scudamore, in little laye-matters would steale opportunity to serve some friends turns ... because none of these (neere and deere Ladies) durst intermeddle so farre in matters of Common-wealth'.[30] He did not understand the influence these ladies wielded, though he later added in the margin that they were 'a Trinity of Ladies able to worke miracles'. Blanche also ignored him when drawing up her final will of 1589. However, eventually she relented and in a codicil left him the bequest of £100 (c.£12,500 now) which she had originally left to his wife, calling him 'my cousin' (meaning kinsman).[31] It is perhaps significant that his bequest came immediately before her admonition that if any beneficiary tried to contest her will, or troubled her executors, then that person would not receive anything. Mentioning Rowland may have brought to Blanche's mind his combative personality.

His enthusiasm for the military life was dampened by his experiences but it was not entirely extinguished. He continued his story saying: 'After it pleased God to give mee recovery, I resolved for the Lowe-countrey-warres [the Netherlands] againe.'[32] However, he was diverted on his journey by meeting a country gentlewoman who had a manor and an over-shot mill, which, he claimed, awakened his interest in estate improvements. This reminiscence focusing less on the attributes of the girl than on her property, suggests that Rowland was more interested now in an alternative life-style. The army's attractions had somewhat diminished for him and he was actively seeking an heiress, a typical business arrangement among the propertied classes of the period to obtain ownership of a house and an income source from a mill. This fortuitously coincided with another advantageous marriage in the family for by 1579 Blanche, with the undoubted help of Robert Hopton, had arranged the betrothal of Rowland's cousin Katherine with Robert Knollys. In 1579 all the children were still minors and Hopton still held their estates by right of his deceased wife. Katherine and Robert Knollys did not marry until 1583 or 1584; the delay was probably due to legal matters perhaps involving the estates.

Blanche's position at the royal court helped to facilitate the advancement of relations and she had appointed Katherine to be her attendant. All the Knollys brothers were prominent courtiers and their father held various posts including, in 1566, that of Treasurer of the Queen's Chamber. As Robert Knollys' first wife had been the queen's cousin, he certainly took seriously the prestige of his second wife's connection to Blanche. In 1584 Rowland's own sister, Catherine, became the second wife of Sir Henry Gate, who had worked closely with another of Blanche's nephews during the Northern Rebellion. (On 14 November 1569 the earls of Northumberland and Westmoreland led their followers to Durham Cathedral to celebrate the Catholic mass and instigated a rebellion. Their revolt was soon contained. Blanche's nephew, John Vaughan, was involved with the government's response.)[33] The royal court was a small, tight-knit circle of people who knew each other and were often connected to each other by marriage and descent. Blanche had close relations and connections with the families of Herbert, Knollys, Knyvett and Burghe, the Barons of Gainsborough.[34] She was cousin to Sir William Cecil, Lord Burghley, the Queen's Lord Treasurer and her friends included Lady Cobham, Lady Stafford and Sir Christopher Hatton, Lord Chancellor in 1587. Rowland certainly knew the potential value of such a network for in *His Booke* he claimed that he was 'kin to most of the Old Nobility ... I can light on a Howard, a Herbert, a Somerset, a Carew, or a Knowles [Knollys]'.[35]

The Herberts, a noble family, were particularly important as patrons. Blanche was the only living family member of Rowland's and Elizabeth's grandparents' generation. No wonder the family kept close contact with her for she was now the most closely related to the Herberts. Blanche's great-grandmother was the sister of Sir William Herbert, later the 1st earl of Pembroke (first Herbert creation). This Sir William's wife was from the Devereux family, later created earls of Essex. Henry Tudor, the future King Henry VII, was at one time their ward at Raglan Castle. Sir William's eventual heir was a grand-daughter who married into the Somerset family of the earls of Worcester. The Pembroke estates were later returned to the grandson of one of Sir William's illegitimate sons who became the earl of Pembroke (second Herbert creation). Therefore, through Blanche and her generation, Rowland and his wife, Elizabeth, could claim long-standing family connections with the earls of Pembroke, the earls of Worcester and, more remotely, with the earls of Essex, one of whom became the step-son of Robert Dudley earl of Leicester, as well as the locally important Scudamore, Stradling and Parry families.

Tudor family connections were all-important. So Katherine, in 1579,[36] one of the cousins who had been brought up in the household[37] of Watkyn and Joan, could be advantageously betrothed.[38] She was anyway living at the royal court with Blanche. In 1580 Rowland was probably back home in Bredwardine, convalescing from the disease he had caught in the Irish Wars and contemplating his future. He was educated, well-built, a sportsman, certainly sociable and confident, loyal and an optimist, though, on the debit side, wilful, obstinate – an opportunist with a tendency to be aggressive when matters did not suit him. He also became increasingly bored during the two years he lived in his father's house, tired of doing nothing and 'fearing [his] fortunes had beene over-throwne'[39] in leaving the military. However, probably also at home in Bredwardine was the unwed Elizabeth, Katherine's sister. Her future was also under consideration. Rowland and Elizabeth therefore would have had the opportunity to become more closely acquainted. More pragmatically, it is possible that her brother William, unmarried and with no children, was already ill. If this was the case, then the old idea tentatively harboured by Watkyn and Joan to partly re-unite the Parry estate, with additions from the Vaughan estate, was an additional incentive. Rowland would have seen the possibility of owning land and a house through marriage to Elizabeth.

In 1582 they were married, probably in Bredwardine church. Marriage, when Rowland was about 24 years old, was a turning point in his life. He had experienced the intrigues and gossip of the royal court, and enjoyed the excitements of London. He had known the company and leadership of men in the army on active service. Now, young, active and ambitious, he was married and looking for a new role to temper the often dull and monotonous return to rural life. There were, of course, new responsibilities. Elizabeth expected him to adopt the role of a country gentleman, managing the tenants such as the miller, who like all traditional millers could be a sharp dealer, and keeping an eye on the Newcourt estate which would be part of Elizabeth's Parry inheritance. However, Rowland had not entirely given up on his military career and remained exercised by 'what was best to be done to preserve my reputation with my martiall companions, and with-all to give contentment to my vertuous and loving wife',[40] suggesting that Elizabeth admired a man of social standing and perhaps, in particular, one with a military reputation.

A year later, in 1583, William Vaughan, Elizabeth's brother, died soon after he came of legal age.[41] This must have caused mixed feelings, for his death was a great sadness for his sisters and the family, but from a business point of view his sisters were his co-heiresses. Rowland could hope, in due course, to inherit a share from his parents, but Elizabeth, in 1583, inherited and co-owned her family's estate with her sister Katherine. From Rowland's point of view his marriage to Elizabeth was the starting point of his life as the squire of Bacton in the Golden Valley of Herefordshire for he now owned property in right of his wife. It was reasonable that Rowland should think his future was assured, comfortable in a house he owned, and free of financial worries.

Unfortunately, this assumption did not prove true. The first difficulty was that the couple may not have been able to move immediately into Newcourt as the will of Elizabeth Whitney on 10 December 1583, shows it was leased to Whitney and Vaughan relatives.[42] Then they realised that Elizabeth's paternal grandfather, Sir Roger Vaughan, had not been a wealthy man when he died in 1571. He is said to have left goods and chattels worth no more than £100 (c.£17,400 now), which were completely overshadowed by his debts of £2,000 (c.£348,000 now), resulting in family members becoming both homeless and destitute.[43] In 1581, the year before Rowland's and Elizabeth's marriage, the ever-dependable Blanche Parry had stepped in to salvage the family estates and return them to William, Elizabeth's brother. Unfortunately for all concerned, this solution was rendered useless by William's early death in 1583. Blanche, now in her 70s, was saddled with the whole ghastly problem of paying off the accumulated debts by mortgages and sales. Fortunately she could, and did, call on the support of her cousin and friend the powerful Lord Burghley.[44]

Among Sir Roger's rash mistakes had been his purchase of the Bronllys and Cantrecelly parts of the earl of Leicester's estate without paying him the full £1,800 purchase price. As Lord Leicester sold the land to raise money, this manoeuvre obliged him to mortgage it to Sir Thomas Gresham of London, the founder of the Royal Exchange. It was a litigious age and Rowland, easily aroused, was not averse to fighting law-suits however shaky or drawn-out they were.[45] As a result, in 1583, Rowland and Robert Knollys, Katherine's future husband, also young and inexperienced, were immediately drawn into legal battles to retain at least some of these Welsh estates near Talgarth, the situation being further complicated by a cousin's claim.[46] When in 1584 Rowland and Robert Knollys attempted to recover the manors of Bronllys and Cantrecelly from Sir Thomas Gresham, his widow contemptuously dismissed them as 'young gentlemen altogether unacquainted with the law'. However, the two men may have found that they enjoyed legal disputes for in the same year both engaged in a successful lawsuit, in which they were joined by Elizabeth and Katherine, to obtain part of the manor of Talgarth itself, probably in order to extend their property bases. Further, in 1585, Rowland joined with Robert Knollys against his benefactress Blanche Parry and Hugh Powell of New Sarum concerning lands in Brecon.[47] Knollys maintained that he had never intended to offend Mistress Blanche, his wife's great-aunt. One consequence was the commissioning by the practical, meticulous Blanche of a detailed map of Llangorse Lake so the land disputes could be the more easily understood when examined in London. The outcome of this plethora of law-suits over the Welsh lands is uncertain but Knollys felt sufficiently secure to make his seat at Porthaml from where he represented Breconshire as an MP from 1589 to 1604.[48] Most of these law-suits concerned lands, estates and inheritance. They cost money but if they had been successful Rowland gambled that he would have accumulated additional finance.

Within a short time of Rowland's and Elizabeth's marriage one problem was happily resolved for they were finally able to move into Newcourt. Here the following year, in about January 1583, a son, John, was born to them.[49] Newcourt, a comfortable gentleman's family home, was an oak panelled house built in 1452, but now with a porch giving it a fashionable E shape, and attractive gardens.[50] The derelict hillside castle that it replaced was utilised as the courtyard entrance but it is doubtful if they had the time or resources for further rebuilding for surely Rowland would have trumpeted the fact when describing the visionary grand house he planned for himself as governor of his 'Commonwealth'.[51]

An important attraction of Newcourt was its deer park. As deer parks could only be allowed by the Crown, it was a sign of honour from the monarch and therefore conferred enormous

Fig. 2.9 View across the Golden Valley from the site of Newcourt.
Nothing survives of the original manor. The present day Newcourt Farm is in the foreground,
with Morehampton in the distance across the valley.

status on the owner. This was enhanced by the way it was utilised. Visitors progressed north of the house to enter through the lodge, whose position is still recorded in 'Lodge Fields'.[52] The approach road then took them south towards the house with the deer park laid out on their right, the western side, and the beautiful Golden Valley on their left, the eastern side. The lay-out was designed to enhance the status of the owner. After such a traverse visitors were expected to be impressed and presumably were less inclined to argue with the owner who could command such luxury. Newcourt's deer park, estimated to have been of several hundred acres, was shown on Saxton's 1577 map made under the patronage of Lord Burghley (map 2.1). A 1624 survey[53] described the park: 'The land ... lies within Newcourt Park. ... It joins to the park pale at a stile entering into the said park from a tenement ... near St. Margaret's: and from the said stile it follows along a far green broad meare from oak to oak, where the pale did sometime stand, to be discerned by the burrs & knots of the said trees that have grown over the holes where the paling rails were let into the said trees: and at length it follows a great bank reared up on both sides to a little brook or gutter of water, which brook does bound it on the east to the corner ... [of] the house ...'.[54] Although the deer park needed attention, requiring money that Rowland could not afford, he was nevertheless pleased that such a prestige feature was attached to Newcourt.

Elizabeth died at Newcourt, *c.*1588 when John was 4 or 5 years old.[55] She had given Rowland another son, William, a Vaughan family name, and possibly other children.[56] It seems likely that Rowland was very upset at losing her as he had recorded that he wanted 'to give contentment to my vertuous and loving wife', suggesting that he did love her. Rowland did not marry again, to Anne Jones, until *c.*1593-95.[57] Elizabeth had evidently supported him by encouraging his home-labours but she also drew a homily from him that: 'I obeyed her will, as many doe, and many miseries do ensew [ensue] thereby',[58] suggesting a more complicated relationship. Elizabeth is revealed as having her own firm opinions, despite fulfilling the meek wifely role of the time. Although only the first of Rowland's three wives, he remembered her with fondness as the mother of his first two sons, as well as bringing him ownership of land and property.

3 THE SUITABILITY OF 'THE GILDEN VALE' FOR A SYSTEM OF WATERWORKS

This chapter looks at the farming systems that had prevailed in the Golden Valley in the years up to the Elizabethan period, before considering systems of water management practised primarily by abbey granges in the preceding centuries and more recent Tudor systems of which Rowland might have been aware. It then considers the suitability of the topography and the geology of the Golden Valley for the implementation of a water management system.

Medieval and Tudor farming in the Golden Valley

The remnants of the medieval open-field system in the Golden Valley have been mapped by Rosamund Skelton as part of the Golden Valley Archaeological Survey in the 1980s[1] (Map 3.1).

The basic three-field system involved a rotation of wheat or rye, followed by a spring-sown crop of barley, oats, peas, beans or vetches and then a year of fallow (where the ground was left

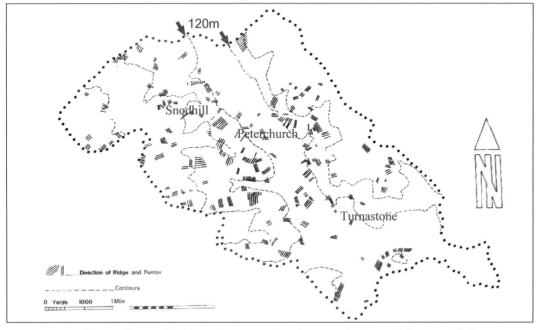

Map 3.1 Golden Valley Archaeological Survey: distribution of ridge and furrow. (Skelton, 1983. All maps from Skelton are Crown Copyright, Dept of Work and Pensions, © 1983)

uncultivated in order to restore its fertility). The fields themselves were divided into furlong strips, which were subdivided into long thin 'ridges' each under the control of a family or individual. These were redistributed, or ownership continued, annually after harvest to ensure each family had the same advantages of soil type and drainage. In areas outside this system of open fields, with its strips of ridge and furrow, the land would be common grazing and woodland. The open field system of agriculture in the Welsh borderland and Herefordshire had a relatively short life, and is poorly documented. In the late middle ages villagers started to rationalise the field strips by purchase or exchange. Informal enclosure had been a feature in the Golden Valley in the 16th century and Rowland himself enclosed land to give him better control over grazing and hay meadows as part of a more intensive system of pastoral farming. This system involved regular-shaped fields that were marked by boundaries of woodland, ditches or hedges.

From the Skelton map it is evident that the remnants of the Anglo-Saxon three-field system, which remain as ridge and furrow elements in the landscape, are concentrated on the slopes above the 120 metre contour. These are most common between Peterchurch and Dorstone, which are outside the areas associated with Rowland's waterworks. The ridge and furrow do not always follow the contours, but run up and down the slope defining the land ploughed by teams of oxen to create open-fields which had a mix of arable and fallow grazing strips in small fields and fragmented ownership. Exceptionally, there is a concentration of ridge and furrow in the floor of the Dore valley in the fields around Poston Court farm, at Turnastone and the lower slopes of Shegear and Cothill farms. The distance between the ridge and furrow varied from 3 to 11 metres, mostly around 7 metres.

Significantly, there is little other evidence for these field systems in the area covered by Rowland's water management system, but the evidence may have been lost by subsequent alluvial deposition in the valley floor. It is also possible that what has been thought to be ridge and furrow around Poston Court may represent a form of 'bedworks' (as described in Chapter 4) created in Rowland Vaughan's scheme for distributing water over the flat-bottomed alluvial plain.

Another feature of the agricultural system at the time that Rowland was developing his waterworks was the pattern of grazing of Ryeland sheep, first developed by the Cistercians in the 12th century. In the Tudor period the transition from an 'open-field' system to the development of individual ownership and successive enclosure of land formed part of the drive for agricultural innovation and the redistribution of land in the 50 years following the dissolution of the monasteries in 1536-39. This transfer of land and farming practice was particularly important in the Golden Valley, where the Cistercian Dore Abbey had managed a group of 'grange farms' for sheep rearing on 'ryelands' – arable fields used for grazing after the harvest.

In order to keep the fine wool of the sheep, for which they are most famous, it was necessary for the sheep to be run in covered pens so they were sheltered from the cold at night. This practice survived into the 19th century at Cothill Farm, a name derived from the word 'sheepcot' which was described by the 18th-century agricultural improver, William Marshall, as deriving from the traditional Herefordshire practice of 'cotting sheep'. In this process sheep were moved from the meadows at night and housed on the 'ground floor of a building large enough to allow each sheep a space of a square yard'[2] and where they were fed hay, barley, and pea haulm. The manure was cleaned out once a year and spread over the arable land. In the days before artificial fertilizers, sheep were highly valued for their dung and it was the usual practice to fold sheep in the open arable land, moving the hurdles steadily uphill to ensure the whole field was evenly manured. Folding sheep at night had the added benefit of reducing the risk of liver disease from their exposure to liver fluke carried by snails in cold, dew-laden pastures. For the same reason, sheep were removed from the meadows in early May and any water-meadows were shut up for hay after a brief watering.

The grazing of cattle was also a common feature of the Welsh borderlands, any water-meadows providing cattle grazing in late summer and early autumn. Over many generations the climate and clay soils of Herefordshire meant that the main crop was grass, so the cattle that came out of the area were well adapted to an almost exclusively grass diet and therefore they were cheaper to keep.

During the late 16th century the main land uses were arable (often over 50% on Golden Valley estates), very little permanent pasture or grass leys, and most grazing from mixed wood pasture, the aftermath grazing of arable crops, and the hay meadows. Significantly, where water-meadows were found naturally in river valleys, the financial returns from hay and grazing of meadows was up to three times greater per acre than arable production. If there had not been any rainfall in the period before hay meadows were to be cut, irrigating the fields a few days in advance of haymaking would ensure that the land did not overly dry out during the week-long harvesting, encouraging new growth on the aftermath which might either yield a second hay crop or offer fresh grazing sooner than would have been the case.

Thus there was a great incentive for the development of managed water-meadows which would increase yields and natural fertility through irrigation and siltation; give market advantage for early lambs; reduce winter feed requirements for cattle; and increase stocking levels as part of a more sustainable mixed agriculture.

Tudor farming systems
The early systems of Tudor grassland management have been identified by Carolina Lane[3] in her analysis of Tudor farming practice, where she argues that during the 16th century land used for grazing and hay crops was not specifically cultivated for that purpose. Very little fodder was grown for winter feeding, but in those areas where there was both arable and livestock rearing, livestock would be fed on the stubble of arable crops and whatever land could be grazed. This was an extensive system and required large tracts of land for grazing with low carrying capacities for livestock. She identified six kinds of land used for feed for livestock: wastes at edges of villages or parishes; the ground cover on fallow fields, which may have had a catch crop of vetches; the stubble left on arable lands after the harvest; woodland pasture which were browsed/grazed for fruits and herbaceous plants; natural meadows, which are lands that border running water and are liable to flood; and pastures, which are drier, and which may or may not form part of the commons. The types of vegetation available for grazing were those which grew naturally in the particular environment, with the possible addition of vetches. In some cases farmers added marl, lime, manures and vegetable wastes to improve the grass leys.

However, pressures on arable production during the 16th century, with the recovery of population and the increasing demands for food, resulted in three distinct periods of change in grassland management. Firstly, by the 1540s pressures on land were such that leys, which before had simply been excess land which was allowed to regain its fertility, were used as grazing lands. Then, about the 1570s these grass leys became systematically used and were ploughed up and either left to regain a sward or used for growing grains and other crops in rotation. Thirdly, by the 1590s different patterns of grass management emerged and farmers began regular sowing of hay grass dust and seeds of plants desired to form better swards.

Thus by the end of the 16th century ploughing up of leys and sowing of seeds for swards was more common, and it is in this context that we can see the economic incentive for the development of more managed grasslands, the need to reclaim poorly drained lowland pasture to ensure regular crops of hay, and the benefits of water-meadows to increase livestock numbers by providing winter fodder and an early bite for sheep during the hungry gap in early spring. If the growth of the meadow grass could be brought forward at the end of winter the number of cattle and flocks of sheep could be increased. If the flooding were repeated in summer, a second harvest of hay might be obtained. It is in this context that we should evaluate the incentives for Rowland to extend the area under irrigation in the Golden Valley.

The history of water-meadows

Evidence for the development of grassland management practices in the 16th century[4] as identified by Carolina Lane can be found in the works of two 'agricultural improvers' of the period: Master Fitzherbert[5] and John Norden.[6]

Fitzherbert refers to pasture and meadow management on different kinds of land and recognised that some pastures may previously have been used as arable, but he did not indicate how to improve such pasture lands. He did, however, recognise the importance of draining and ploughing some pasture in the spring to improve the grass mix for hay. He also recognised the importance of setting land aside to recover as leys. Winter grazing would be found on the different types of land used for corn, hay, and common pasture.

John Norden's work contained what appears to be the first suggestion that the care of pastures and meadows should be part of a systematic rotation. Improvement of the land was stressed throughout his book. He classified as pasture all tillable land and thus upland meadows were included as pasture. He distinguished between naturally wet meadows as 'meadows, the cause of whose goodness is the soyle, and ouer-flowing with the most muddy water' and man-made water-meadows. He gave little advice on water management in meadows but encouraged the management of pasture, distinguishing between two forms: the rejuvenating of meadow land, including letting it become grazing ground, and ploughing it up and sowing seed. Meadows which had become weakened by too much cutting of hay could be left as pasture for several years or spread with manures and 'fat soil'.

Wetter lowland meadows could produce up to three times more hay than the dry upland meadows[7] and therefore every incentive existed to extend the area of wet meadow by irrigation. In upland areas like the Golden Valley the upland meadows and the gentler hillsides below were irrigated using artificial rills and leats, formed by taking channels off dammed streams and led along contours, to supply mill ponds, watering pools and farms and then to convey water to the highest point of the grassland where the manure-enriched waters were caused to spill over their banks down the slopes. These leat-grounds were superior to the dry pasture.

Further downstream, irrigation sought to modify natural flooding. The limited control of natural flooding and forms of irrigation in England can be traced back into the middle ages. In their article on the origins of water-meadows (areas of land where the quality and quantity of grassland has been improved for hay production through deliberate water management), Hadrian Cook and colleagues[8] point to the emphasis placed on the mowing for fodder, which still forms an important distinction between meadows and grazing pastures. In practice, watered meadows would provide both pasture and a mown hay crop. 'Flood meadows' are simply areas of low-lying ground prone to natural flooding on alluvial river flood plains. The natural flooding can dress the meadow with silts and nutrients, but flood meadows require slow moving water, not rapidly flowing flood water, to discharge the suspended nutrients. Once the benefits of natural flooding were recognised the next step was to manage the water flow.

Early systems for managing water-meadows used the technique of 'floating upwards' in which a meadow is flooded by controlling water at the point of exit back into the river. In this method the water was simply ponded back behind some barrier, but ran the risk of producing stagnant water conditions which could prove toxic to grass. True irrigation involves controlled floating, with a moving film of water. This method was developed by Rowland to enable greater management of the floodwaters so as to maintain a continuous flow of shallow water by the use of trenches and graded fields.

The Cistercians and water management

The possible influence of Cistercian farming practices on the early development of water-meadows has been identified by Cook and colleagues.[9] In the view of these authors, the 'floating' or artificial irrigation of water-meadows was an innovation that predated Rowland's times, and they suggest there is good evidence that irrigation (in some form or another) was already under-stood and practised on at least a limited scale by the start of the 16th century.

They recognise that some of the most influential examples of water management practice in the middle ages were the sophisticated early medieval Cistercian schemes at Clairvaulx on the river Aube in France and at Rievaulx in Yorkshire. They also noted a 'well developed system of leats associated with a mill but also with areas of meadow land ... within the monastic precinct' at Dore Abbey. Our own researches have also identified the importance of Buildwas Abbey in Shropshire to the development of water management schemes in the Marches. The records of other monastic houses, especially in the north of England, suggest elements of water manage-ment consistent with meadow irrigation including Bolton Priory and Fountains Abbey. R.A. Donkin[10] found references to water-meadows in 12th- and 13th-century records of many other Cistercian properties in Yorkshire and elsewhere.

Of particular note for this study is the evidence for a form of water-meadow flooding at Buildwas Abbey in Shropshire. The basic principles of water-meadow management in this scheme would have been widely adopted in other Cistercian houses, and Rowland would have been familiar with some of these features at Dore Abbey. Historic England (online Heritage Gateway)[11] has recently published an extract from the 'Water meadows of Buildwas Abbey' which gives a full description of the waterworks in the abbey precinct:

> To the west of the stream which forms the western boundary of the abbey precinct, and covering an area of c.6 ha., are the remains of a system of water meadows. These comprise a number of rectangular fields, each of which is bounded by shallow channels averaging 2 m wide. Water would have been fed into the channels from a source to the south, and controlled by sluices to allow selective irrigation.
>
> The surplus water would have fed from the channels into a central drain which runs along the south edge of the meadows, before turning north to discharge into a substantial canal. This is orientated roughly east-west, and cuts across the neck of the river meander

forming the north edge of the meadows. This well-defined channel is *c*.250 m long by 14 m wide and 2 m deep, and is flanked on both sides by levee banks 8 m wide and 0.5 m high.

At the east end the channel branches into two, the northern and smaller of the two branches probably acting as an outflow, curving north-east to discharge into the river. The southerly channel curves south-east and fades after *c*.80m on the edge of the possible mere west of the main fishpond complex.

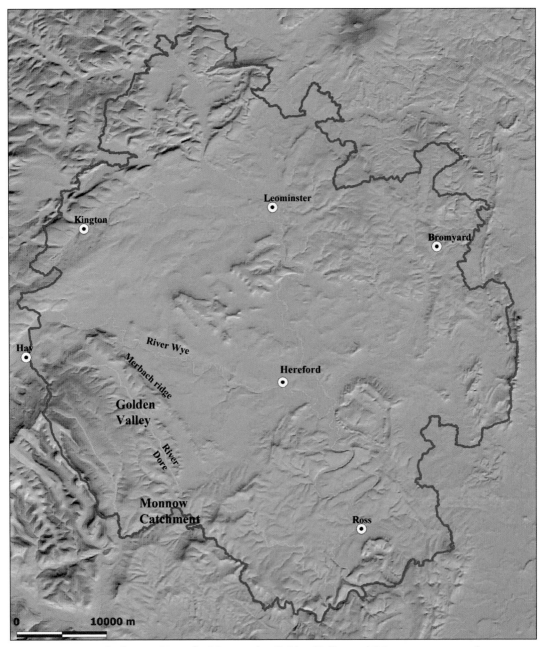

Map 3.2 Relief map of Herefordshire – the Golden Valley and Monnow river catchment.

The topography of the Golden Valley

The land uses discussed in the first part of this chapter were those to be found in the Golden Valley and the adjacent slopes at the time that Rowland was developing his waterworks. The land uses would have been patchy and broken up to reflect the natural advantages of slope, soils, water distribution and access – themselves resulting from the topography and geology of the area – creating a diverse pattern of grazing, arable and woodland.

The setting for Rowland's 'water-workes' in the Golden Valley of south-west Herefordshire embraces both the lowlands of the river Wye, and the valleys of the Monnow river catchment in the borderlands of the Welsh Marches, as they drain the lower slopes of the Black Mountains. This complex of rivers includes the river Dore, draining the Golden Valley, the Olchon, Escley and Dulas brooks, and the river Monnow.

The location and characteristic ridge and valley relief of the Welsh Marches and the Golden Valley are illustrated in Map 3.2. The image shows how the river Dore, running from north-west to south-east in the Golden Valley, joins the Monnow and is separated from the Herefordshire plain. The rivers help form a diversity of landscape types which Rowland would have experienced as a child growing up in Bredwardine and Moccas in the Wye valley, and climbing over the Merbach ridge into the 'Gilden Vale' as described in Saxton's map of 1577 (see Map 2.1). Rowland was impressed by the beauty of the 'Golden Vale' which he describes as 'the Lombardy of Herefordshire, the Garden of the old Gallants ...'.[12]

The transition from the rich pastoral and arable lower slopes of the Slough brook and river Dore lowlands, to the 'bocage' pockets of hedgerows and managed upland grazing below the Black Mountains is illustrated in Fig. 3.1. This view was also echoed by the historian and topographer William Camden writing about Herefordshire at the end of the 16th century, when he commented that 'for the three W's, Wheat, Wool and Water it yieldeth to no shire in England'.[13] He also describes the slopes which border the Golden Valley: 'the hills which encompass it on both sides are clothed with woods; under the woods lie cornfields on each hand; and under those fields lovely and fruitful meadows. In the middle between them, glides a clear and crystal river Dore.' Camden's representation of the valley in 1586 is perhaps a simplification of the diverse land use and farming landscape at the time that Rowland developed his waterworks there, but it provides a framework for understanding the changes over the last 400 years.

Fig. 3.1 The Golden Valley rising to the Black Mountains

The fragment of John Speed's map of 1610 (Map 3.3) illustrates the general character of this part of Herefordshire at that time. The river valleys and upland ridges as they rise to the 'Hatterell Hylls' on the west (the eastern ridge of the Black Mountains), are the source of the streams flowing into the 'Gilden Vale' and Herefordshire plain. The course of the Dore, as it passes through the areas occupied by Rowland's estates at Poston Court, Turnastone and Newcourt, is marked by a distinctive feature of the 16th century – the palisades enclosing the deer parks at Newcourt, where Rowland first developed his waterworks, and across the river Dore at Morehampton. These enclosures for hunting deer were distinctive features of the Tudor landscape and reflected the status of Rowland at this time as a man of means. The valley then passes through the lands of Dore Abbey, a Cistercian foundation which also had distinctive impacts on the landscape.

Map 3.3 Fragment of John Speed's map 1610 – the Gilden Vale in south-west Herefordshire.

The local drift, soils and solid geology of the river Dore

The local drift and solid geology of the river Dore below Peterchurch (Map 3.4) is characterised by a valley bottom partially covered by glacial drift and river alluvial deposits some 500-1,000m wide and 120m above sea level. The valley floor is abutted by relatively steeply rising slopes of Lower Old Red Sandstone of the Raglan Mudstone Formation (Rg), made up of mudstones and siltstones. These are overlain by outcrops of Bishop's Frome Limestone (BFL) where the limestone has been exposed. The adjacent uplands are formed of Upper Old Red Sandstone of

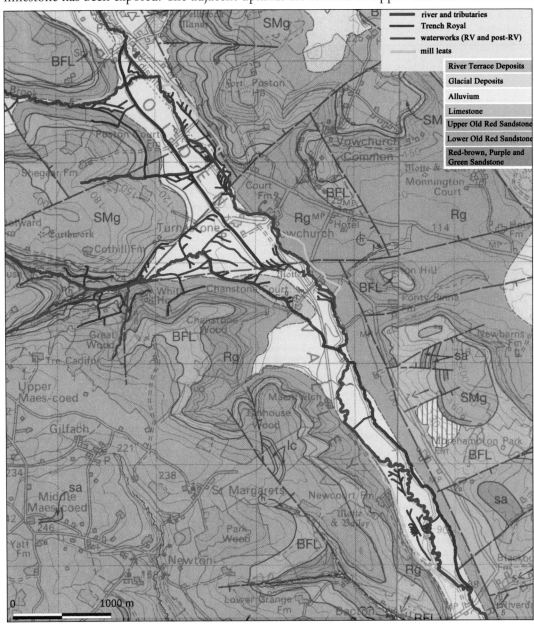

Map 3.4 Solid and drift geology and Rowland's waterworks.
(Geological Survey E & W Sheet 214 Talgarth)

29

the St Maughans Formation (SMg). These are also mudstones and siltstones with narrow beds of red-brown, purple and green sandstones (sa). These ridges run for approximately 9 kilometres in a south-east/north-west direction on either side of the valley floor and rise to form a series of rolling, more rounded sandstone ridges covered with heavier clays on plateau land at 225-300m above sea level.

The boundaries between the permeable limestone and the less permeable mudstones and siltstones are often marked by springs. The uplands are cut by several steep running streams, including the Trenant brook and the Slough brook, which form wider valley bottoms where they enter the Dore valley at right angles.

The valley floor is partially covered in glacial drift deposits, marking the extent of glaciation in the valley just below Peterchurch. These include undifferentiated sandy tills and 'head deposits' of boulder clays and rubble. Below the glacial 'standstill' south of Peterchurch, the valley bottom may formerly have been covered by a glacial melt-water lake which formed behind the terminal moraines blocking the entrance to the Golden Valley from the Wye Valley at the Batcho.[14] These moraines also diverted the course of the Grey river valley. Today, the Golden Valley floor is overlaid with fertile 'alluvium' – a mix of sand, silts and clays deposited by rivers and the melt-water lake.

The soils of Herefordshire have been classified by Burnham,[15] who distinguishes the upland soils as forming generally mixed permeability soils made up of reddish acid brown soils with friable fine sandy loams which, importantly, are generally free from subsoil water-logging. Because the valley floor soils are generally free-draining, they can benefit from the neutralising effect of the calcareous deposits found in suspension in the streams which flow over low permeability bedrock in the uplands.

These soil conditions are important to the development of Rowland's waterworks because they have generally good infiltration characteristics and allow artificial floodwaters to sink into the valley floor and disperse relatively quickly – the balance between irrigation and drainage is therefore maintained. Heavier clay lands would not benefit so much from water-meadow irrigation schemes as they would become waterlogged and sour. In addition, the limestone outcrops on the west of the valley provide permeable aquifers in the beds of nodular limestone or 'cornstone' or where hard calcareous marls occur, which provide calcium-rich deposits and silts in suspension to flow over the lowland pastures to increase fertility and reduce the acidity of the soils. Given these natural advantages, the waterworks were developed to manage the winter and summer flows of water to improve the farmland for agriculture, reduce soil erosion, extend the growing season in the spring and summer and increase yields.

Natural drainage in the Golden Valley
The Dore valley between Peterchurch and Bacton is of variable width and extends over 6 kilometres, with tributary streams which are more numerous where they rise from the west compared to the eastern valley slopes. The gathering grounds of the Trenant brook have tributary streams which rise in the St Maughans Formation sandstones, before cutting steeply through the Bishops Frome limestone. They then flow more gently across glacial deposits of sandy tills, and undifferentiated boulder clays, before cutting a steep, straight course through the Raglan Mudstones to enter the Dore valley. The steep fall in the course of the Trenant brook has also been used by watermills.

The headwaters of the Slough brook fall steeply over the St Maughans Formation sandstones, before cutting more gently through the limestone and mudstone formations and across a mix of glacial head deposits of sand, silt and clay, which formed the site for a series of water channels following the contours and feeder channels for a series of ponds and mill leats. The valley of the Slough brook then cuts back into the sandstone ridge to form an extensive fan-shaped outwash plain over 1,000 metres from west to east to form a wide deposit of alluvial sand, silt and clay and a broad alluvial fan deposit on land occupied today by Turnastone and Chanstone Court farms.

Below Chanstone Court an unnamed stream cuts back into the adjacent uplands to broaden the valley floor with alluvial silt deposits. The Dore valley bottom then narrows below the site of Newcourt on the west and the gently rising limestone slopes of Morehampton Grange on the east. In the section between Newcourt, and Abbeydore a series of short streams feed the Dore from the adjacent eastern slopes.

Climate and irrigation in the Dore valley

The annual rainfall measures show a significant shift from 110-120cm in the uplands to 75-80cm in the Dore valley. However, the most important characteristics of the rainfall patterns for irrigation in the valley are its seasonal variability between winter and summer, and its relative peaks and troughs as the runoff combines with rocks of different permeability. River flow patterns are not dominatingly influenced by seasonal contrasts in rainfall as, on average, it is fairly evenly distributed throughout the year with a more marked tendency towards an autumn/ winter maximum in the western catchments of the Dore. By contrast, seasonal variations in temperature and sunshine amounts ensure that evaporation losses are heavily concentrated in the summer half-year (April-September). In turn, this imposes a marked seasonality on river flows with maximum flows normally in the winter and minimum flows normally occurring in the summer or autumn.

The mix of low permeable rocks in the adjacent uplands with mixed permeable drift deposits and the limestone aquifers in close proximity in the Dore valley provides a series of advantages for the development of water management irrigation systems. The impermeable uplands produce a series of tributaries falling into the Dore which respond rapidly to rainfall on the adjacent slopes and so provide a highly seasonal flow of water. However, the limestone aquifers help to moderate this flow, absorbing a proportion of the local rainfall during the peak period from November to April in normal years, and discharging lime rich water at springs and seepage zones throughout the year. Through the summer months the system of cracks and higher porosity limestone beds help to determine the storage and transmission characteristics of the run-off in this part of the Dore valley.

The resulting landscape of the Golden Valley

The topography and geology, as worked by man for farming, has resulted in the existing landscape of the Golden Valley and whilst the land-use pattern has changed since the 16th century, the significant structural elements of the uplands and valleys have maintained a strong impact on the diversity of landscape characteristics seen today. Thus we only need to modify what is seen today a little to recreate a picture of the landscape at the time of Rowland Vaughan.

The distinctive characteristics of this part of Herefordshire and the Marches have been identified as a series of landscape types in the Landscape Character Assessment (LCA), a study undertaken by Herefordshire Council in 2004 (revised 2009).[16] The landscape types are defined using natural features – geological, soil types, and topographical – with additional characteristics reflecting man's impact on the environment – land use, settlement pattern and tree cover. Map 3.5 shows the different types of landscape found in the south-west of Herefordshire focusing on the Golden Valley borderlands.

In the LCA study, the main landscape type identified in the floor of the river Dore and adjacent lower slopes is defined as 'Principal Settled Farmlands' (see Fig. 3.2) in which the main characteristics are mixed farming with rolling lowland areas divided by hedgerows, relic commons, scattered farms and small villages. Hop fields, orchards, grazed pastures and arable fields together make up this rich patchwork of land uses. It is a landscape that first became prominent in the 18th and 19th centuries with the agricultural reforms of this period extending arable acreage, grass leys and 3-4 crop rotation patterns. The agricultural innovations of this period were relatively limited in Herefordshire, but more recently the Golden Valley

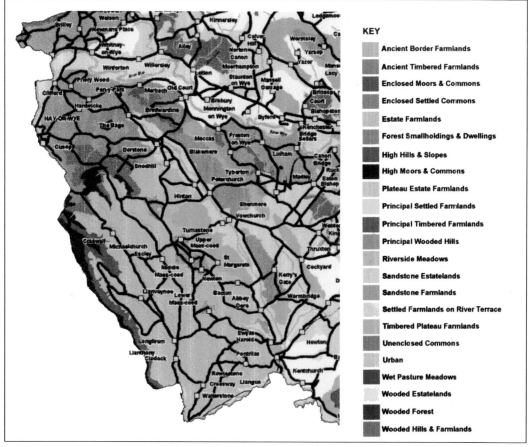

KEY

Ancient Border Farmlands
Ancient Timbered Farmlands
Enclosed Moors & Commons
Enclosed Settled Commons
Estate Farmlands
Forest Smallholdings & Dwellings
High Hills & Slopes
High Moors & Commons
Plateau Estate Farmlands
Principal Settled Farmlands
Principal Timbered Farmlands
Principal Wooded Hills
Riverside Meadows
Sandstone Estatelands
Sandstone Farmlands
Settled Farmlands on River Terrace
Timbered Plateau Farmlands
Unenclosed Commons
Urban
Wet Pasture Meadows
Wooded Estatelands
Wooded Forest
Wooded Hills & Farmlands

Map 3.5 Landscape characteristics in south-west Herefordshire, from the
Herefordshire Landscape Character Assessment (LCA).
(© Herefordshire Council, HER, 2009. Crown Copyright all rights reserved)

Fig. 3.2 Principal settled farmlands

was subject to further change in the post Second World War intensification and specialisation of farming patterns. This has resulted, today, in a predominance of permanent pasture in the lowlands of the river Dore, with some arable.

The more steeply sided hillsides of the Golden Valley have a patchwork of densely wooded, irregular-shaped ancient woodland cover. The hillsides are bisected by deep, wooded stream-lines like the Slough and Trenant brooks, which flow down the western slopes of the valley to join the river Dore. The steepness of the slopes has inhibited clearance for arable use in the past, although they are often interlinked with cleared areas used for pasture and some arable, including remnants of ancient ridge and furrow as has been noted.

The 'ryelands' were a prominent feature of Cistercian sheep farming in the Dore valley and were centred on the valley floor at Dore Abbey and the adjacent slopes where their grange farms extended up the valley. They developed a characteristic mix of grazing pasture and arable before the dissolution of the monasteries in 1536-39. This type of landscape is designated 'Principal Wooded Hills' (Fig. 3.3) in the Herefordshire study and would have been a familiar sight for Rowland and a rich source of timber, grain and grazing.

Fig. 3.3 Principal wooded hills

Fig. 3.4 Ancient border farmlands

Additional features are related to the water flows in the Monnow catchment and the prevalence of natural water-meadows and flooded pasture in the Wye valley. To the west of the Golden Valley in an area encompassing the rivers of the Olchon, Monnow and Escley and Dulas valleys, the landscape is very distinctive and its field patterns are thought to be one of the oldest in the county. They are designated as 'Ancient Border Farmlands' (Fig. 3.4) and described as: 'remote, small scale, pastoral landscapes with dispersed farms and many scattered hedgerow trees, in species-rich hedgerows defining small pockets of grazing in a dramatically rolling topography'. The pattern of small, irregular, often rounded-shaped fields were developed to manage grazing and hay making in fields just below the more extensive grazing in the adjacent upland slopes of the Black Mountains.

The landscape is interspersed with the rich valley bottoms of the Monnow catchment tributaries and isolated tablelands of former, and existing commons on higher ground (250-300 metres above sea level) producing a fairly flat and moderately gentle landform – the 'Enclosed Settled Commons' in the area around Newton St Margaret's. The small to medium sized pastoral fields are divided in a regular pattern and were probably enclosed from common land in the 19th century, as they were still open in the 1842-43 tithe maps. These borderlands and open commons could have been familiar to Rowland as they had economic links to the richer Dore valley.

Rowland would also have recognised two other landscape forms which are found in the Wye valley at Letton and below Moccas and on all the major rivers in Herefordshire. These areas were designated 'Riverside Meadows' and 'Wet Pasture Meadows' in the LCA. The riverside meadows are linear, riverine landscapes associated with flat, generally well defined, alluvial floodplains, in places framed by steeply sided rising ground. They are secluded pastoral landscapes, with meandering tree-lined rivers, flanked by riverside meadows which were defined by hedge and ditch boundaries. They formed extensive areas of meadow, accommodating a degree of annual flooding and habitats tolerant of waterlogged conditions. Other riverside meadows were found in the Castleton (Clifford) area of the Wye Valley and at Winforton just north-west of Bredwardine. However, the natural fertility of the riverside meadows was a great incentive to develop water management systems which used sluices to control and direct the silt-laden flood waters. The Lammas Meadows bordering the river Lugg near Hereford are a good example of traditionally managed riverside meadows, where the cutting for hay and grazing has been continued since medieval times, and 'dole stones' still mark different holders' strips.

The other water landscape found in the Wye and Golden Valleys at the time of Rowland, the 'Wet Pasture Meadows', are flat, poorly drained, low-lying basins which collect water from surrounding low hills. Because of the difficulty of cultivating these soils with such poor drainage, they have not always been economically viable for agricultural improvement and today provide valuable wetland habitats with an element of pastoral farming.

Unimproved, natural water-meadows near to farmland were also a feature of the western edge of the Olchon Valley. They contrast with the open, acidic grasslands found on the hills and give one the characteristic 'upland edge' landscape of the Black Mountains which contrasts with the densely hedged landscapes of the valley. These areas of natural meadows were more evident in the Golden Valley in the 16th century than today, and their conversion to pasture and hay meadows as part of Rowland's waterworks involved both irrigation and drainage systems to manage both flooding and periods of drought.

Land use changes in the Golden Valley

A more detailed analysis of land use in the Golden Valley today is revealed by the aerial survey of land use. In Map 3.6 the land use features have been overlaid with a map of the natural and man-made water features which the Golden Valley Study Group (GVSG) identified as possibly forming the main elements of Rowland's 'water-workes'. The red lines define man-made irriga-tion and drainage channels including both Rowland's and some later works. Rowland's major distributor channel – the Trench Royal – is shown in purple. The natural river and brook flows of the Dore valley are shown in blue. Rowland's system extended for almost 3 kilo-metres from just below Peterchurch to south of Turnastone, with a further 2½ kilometres at Newcourt. Rowland was prevented from extending or joining up the Newcourt system with that at Poston/Whitehouse by the opposition of the owners of the Chanstone estate (Kemp family), who owned the land between. From the aerial survey it is evident that, whilst some fields in the valley floor have been ploughed for arable use, these are concentrated in the area around Chanstone Court, which was not included in Rowland's scheme. However, some fields north of Newcourt have also been ploughed, and may have eroded the waterworks features in this part of the system. The adjacent lower slopes are generally used for permanent pasture and grass leys with areas of ancient woodland.

The modern day land use pattern shows some significant changes from the 1842-43 tithe maps. In the 1840s (see Map 3.7), the riverine lowlands of the river Dore between Peterchurch and Bacton had smaller pockets of arable fields on the valley floor, but a greater extension of arable on the lower slopes rising up to the Slough and the Shegear brooks, including hop yards, roots, and cereals. In the 1840s, therefore, the floor of the valley remained relatively open for grassland and meadow. The land use evidence for remnants of water-meadows is concentrated in the south-east corner of the map around Newcourt, which was the location for Rowland's first waterworks (see the following chapter). Some of the fields on adjacent lower slopes also had extensive areas of orchards and woodland amidst arable and pasture. However, the evidence from place-names on the 1842-43 tithe maps indicates extensive development of water-meadows in this area, as well as the Peterchurch-Turnastone part of the Golden Valley which was the focus of Rowland's second stage of water management development.

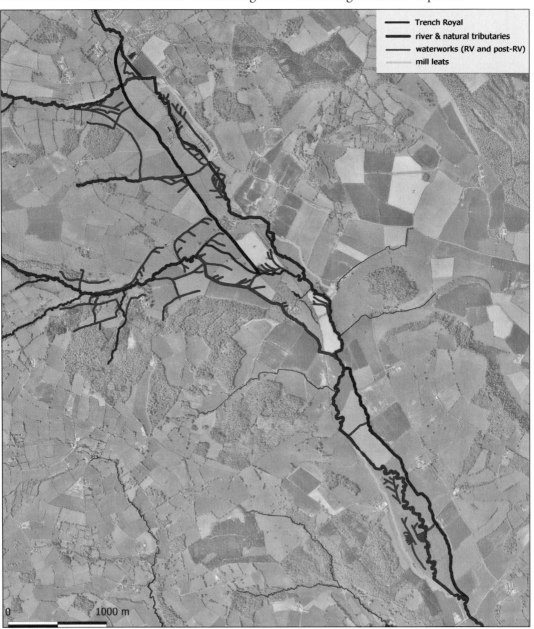

Map 3.6 *Rowland's use of water in the Golden Valley – overlay on aerial survey 2000*

In his article surveying agricultural change in Herefordshire in the 17th and 18th centuries, E.L. Jones[17] notes that there was an exceptionally diverse pattern of land use established in the early 17th century and sustained over a long period. There was no strong movement to enclose or reclaim land for arable production as in the eastern counties. The usual criteria of technological innovation, the extension of arable, drainage of land and the introduction of the four crop rotation of the 'Norfolk system' could not be applied to the pattern of agricultural

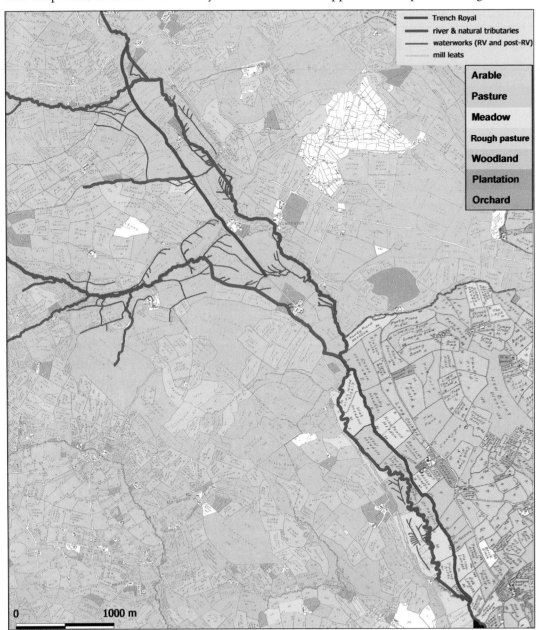

Map 3.7 Rowland Vaughan's use of water in the Golden Valley – overlay on 1842/3 tithe map of land use and field names. (Compiled by Geoff Gwatkin & David Lovelace)

change in the western clay lands and mixed arable and pastoral agricultural systems found in the Golden Valley.

The Golden Valley had already experienced a long process of piecemeal enclosure and adaptation of the medieval open-field system by the 16th century and Rowland secured a more systematic enclosure of the remnants of the open-field system on his estates as he diversified crop and livestock production with the expansion of his water management system in the valley. It is important to note here that Rowland considered that his water management system could bring benefits to pasture and arable fields as well as water-meadows. Clovers were not introduced until the mid-1660s and were used extensively with rye grasses over the next century, but the introduction of grass leys was less common in the Golden Valley, where the value of established pasture and water-meadows was recognised as securing a high density of livestock.

As noted at the beginning of the chapter, in the 13th and 14th centuries the monks at Dore Abbey had been major sheep farmers with a string of nine granges in and close to the Golden Valley, exporting wool overseas.[18] It would seem likely that after the dissolution sheep-farming remained important on the hills flanking the valley, as it still is today, but in Rowland's lifetime there were cattle in the valley fields. He wrote, admittedly fancifully, of keeping 3,000 sheep and 600 cows all the year round as well as cultivating ten plough-lands (1,000 acres). Field-names, deeds and hedgerows recorded in the 19th-century tithe maps and landscape features revealed by aerial photography and digital imaging show that much of the valley was formerly cultivated and grazed in open fields, still surviving in the early 18th century. Open field meadows where tenants shared pasturage rights were a hindrance to improvement schemes and it was simple for a small landowner with few tenants to enclose the fields for improving husbandry, redistributing the land in farms. There is some suggestion that this occurred on the Whitehouse estate and at Monnington Straddle, and on a small scale was practised by Rowland himself. Orchards were another hindrance to improvement schemes. John, 1st Viscount Scudamore of Holme Lacy, the lord of the manor of Dore, is credited with introducing the Redstreak cider apple and cultivating orchards from 1635, but apple trees had long been grown in Herefordshire around farmhouses. But improvement schemes would come with Rowland's waterworks.

4   CISTERCIAN WATERWORKS AT DORE ABBEY
AND LATER DEVELOPMENTS BY ROWLAND AT BACTON

Rowland's marriage in 1582 to his cousin Elizabeth Vaughan brought him to Newcourt at Bacton in the Golden Valley. Chapter 2 has described as much as is known about the house and its accompanying deer park (see also Map 2.1 and Fig. 2.9).

In his pursuit of his waterworks, Rowland, as mentioned earlier, may have been influenced by the water management systems on the Cistercian land at Dore Abbey, adjacent to his property at Newcourt and Bacton.

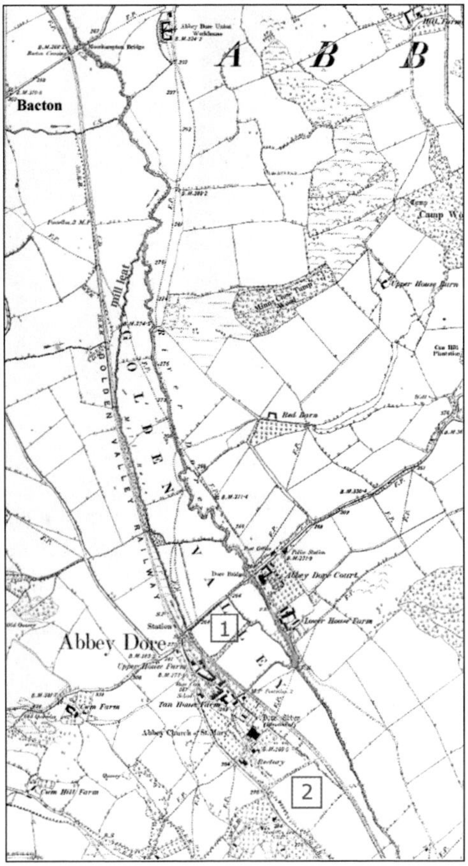

Map 4.1 Abbeydore – mill leats and tails and possible irrigation/drainage channels

The Cistercian water management scheme at Dore Abbey

Dore Abbey was founded in 1147 and managed its agricultural land with the help of 'granges', which were small farms worked by lay brothers under the supervision of the granger, who was responsible to the abbey. These granges usually had a barn (with some accommodation for the lay brothers), animal sheds, and an oratory or place to pray. The buildings were surrounded by a ditch, hedge or wall, and often had a protective gatehouse. Some granges also had watermills, fishponds or dovecots. Dore Abbey was very prosperous and had 17 associated granges, nine of which were in the Golden Valley. Today, there is a cluster of grange farms on the adjacent slopes to the north-west of the abbey at Holling Grange farm, Upper and Lower Grange farms, and 3 kilometres north in the Golden Valley at Morehampton Park farm (grange) and the former Whitewall Grange at Dolward.

The abbey had developed a system of leats associated with a watermill but also with areas of meadowland within the monastic precinct.[1] In Map 4.1 the mill leat can be clearly seen connecting to the river Dore just south of Bacton and extending over

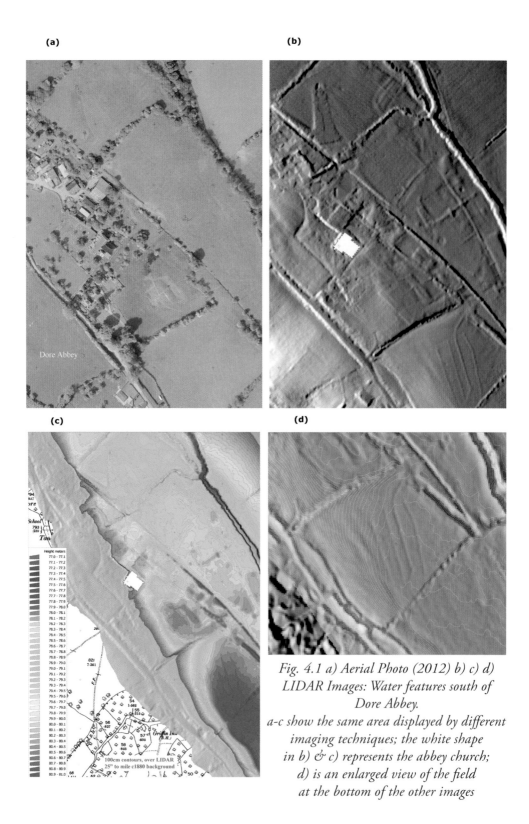

(a)

(b)

Dore Abbey

(c)

(d)

*Fig. 4.1 a) Aerial Photo (2012) b) c) d)
LIDAR Images: Water features south of
Dore Abbey.
a-c show the same area displayed by different
imaging techniques; the white shape
in b) & c) represents the abbey church;
d) is an enlarged view of the field
at the bottom of the other images*

1 kilometre to Abbeydore. In this context, it should be noted that Poston Court mill, located just north of Turnastone and central to Rowland's subsequent waterworks in this area, was established by Dore Abbey in 1291. At Dore Abbey, the mill leat has several tails linking back to the river in the fields north of the abbey (No.1 on Map 4.1), which may have been used to irrigate the meadows. South of the abbey, the aerial survey and LIDAR[2] evidence (Fig. 4.1) clearly demonstrate that a field south of the abbey (No.2 on Map 4.1) could have been used for water-meadow management. Figure 4.1(d) shows evidence of significant fish ponds and water features in the field to the north of the meadow, and deep channels running on the western border of the two fields. From a relatively steep fall from west to east across the field it bottoms out and this area is crossed by a main feeder channel to irrigate the field and a series of drainage channels flowing in a generally north to south direction. The lowest part of the field has a relatively modern field boundary and it is likely that the water-meadows extended south over several fields adjacent to the river Dore.

The low-lying areas form distinctive blue features in the LIDAR image, but the evidence on the aerial survey is less distinct. This scheme has not been dated, but it is possible that Rowland may have been aware of these developments, or himself implemented a new scheme, when he established his waterworks system at Newcourt and, later, the more extensive lands to the north at Whitehouse and Poston.

The principles of Rowland's waterworks scheme
The benefits of irrigation to agriculture are many, and have been summarised in an article by Cook and colleagues.[3] They include: raising the temperature of the soil above 5°C, the point at which germination and growth commences; oxygenation and protection from frost damage encourage early growth; the 'floating' of hay meadows stimulates grass growth by compensating for any soil water deficit in periods of low rainfall; and the dressing of the grass sward with nutrients and calcareous elements (in areas of carboniferous rocks like the Dore valley) enriches the soils and restores the alkaline balance. The result would be an increase in yields of crops (notably grass) and in the numbers of stock that the land could carry. 'Drowning' of the land also led to the elimination of some weeds and mosses and so further improvement of the meadows.

The nature of the waterworks which Rowland developed in the Golden Valley suggests that he understood these benefits and had a sophisticated understanding of the valley, its environment and farming patterns. He used the natural features of seasonal river flows, topography and small changes in the elevation of valley bottom slopes, soils and silt, together with new technologies, to enhance the methods of pastoral and arable farming. He used this knowledge to combine the abundance of water and the richness of the soils to create a water management system which, as Hadrian Cook[4] has pointed out, has two apparently contradictory purposes: it served both to remove excess water from damp soils in order to increase productivity – its drainage function – and to regulate water levels when applied to dry soils during the growing season to increase yields and the frequency of cutting for hay – its irrigation function. In addition, meadow irrigation was also applied in the winter and early spring, when soils are already at their maximum water-carrying capacity (so as to increase soil temperature and give an 'early bite' of grass). In terms of 'drowning the meadows', his system also was designed to manage water levels so as to prevent the soil fertility being washed away. He claimed that his waterworks would transform the Golden Vale to become his 'garden of England'.[5]

Rowland had realised that the benefits of winter irrigation principally arise, not from water penetration, but from the increased temperature it brings to the grass sward. The medieval climatic optimum of the 12th and 13th centuries was followed by the 'little ice age', a cooler period which ran from approximately 1500 to 1850 – coinciding with the main period of water-meadow irrigation.[6] Mean annual temperatures over this period in England are estimated as between 0.2°C and 0.7°C lower than in the mid-20th century, with the effect that the growing season was shorter by one or two months. This impact was more marked during the winter, and the benefits from winter irrigation, in terms of warming the soil, protecting the grass sward from frost and stimulating grass growth, were more marked than they would be today. In the winter, the water control measures provided greater control over the natural flooding of the Dore and its tributaries by building trenches from the tributaries and dispersing the floodwaters over a greater area of the floodplain of the Dore than would have occurred naturally. The waters were then fed back into the river and the deposit of silts was used to restore the fertility of the soil. In the summer, the land was drowned periodically with clean water, which prevented the drying out of the soil in periods of drought and restored the water-meadows with fresh pasture.

In Rowland's system, the water was artificially diverted from rivers, streams and springs and spread over the land. In this it was a development of the earlier system which Rowland would have been aware of, the catchworks system, found on the adjacent slopes of the Slough brook. In this system, water from a spring or stream was led in a channel or 'headmain' along the side of the hill and encouraged to overflow the channel, or pass through openings in its side, so that it spread down the slope before returning to the parent stream or being taken off the land by an artificial tail drain. In some cases a series of parallel 'gutters' was created, to encourage a more even flow of water down the slope; this method was only suitable for areas where there were abundant springs and or hilly terrain with steep, narrow valleys. The early catchwork systems in the upper parts of the Trenant, Shegear and Slough brooks demonstrate these principles (see Chapter 9).

Rowland adapted this system to create a hybrid form of bedworks for drainage and irrigation on the level flood-plain. The bedwork systems were more complex and sophisticated and were used where wide, level floodplains were to be irrigated. A major watercourse would be damned by a weir, immediately above which water was fed by a 'hatch' or sluice into an artificial channel (a 'carriage' or 'main carrier'). This ran roughly parallel with the river, but with a lesser gradient, so that when the water reached the area to be irrigated it was flowing about a metre or more above its natural level. It was then led through smaller carriers and hatches into spade-dug channels which ran along the spines of low ridges or 'beds'. These defined a series of 'panes' which superficially resembled the ridge and furrow earthworks of former open field systems. The water flowed gently down the side of the ridges into drains in the adjacent furrows, and was then returned to the river either directly or via a tail drain.

It has been noted by Kerridge[7] that bedwork systems were more expensive to construct than catchwork, but they were the only way to irrigate meadows where the valley had relatively wide, level floors. Without ridges it would not have been possible to keep the water moving steadily across the surface of low-gradient valley floors, which is essential since the technique requires moving water to maintain the dissolved oxygen to stimulate grass growth. Stagnant water would create anaerobic conditions inimical to grass growth. Costs of construction were considerable: not only was the construction of drains and leats expensive, the sub soils within the area occupied by the meadow were often broken up to some considerable depth in order to improve drainage. In these cases, the turves would need to be removed and replaced. The speed with which the water was taken on and off the field was also critical to the proper 'drowning' of the meadows.

On level valley floors streams and rivers naturally overflow, flooding onto the level ground across their flood-plains. There is some evidence from the 1832 Ordnance Survey[8] map that some areas of natural water-meadows held 'in common' were still extant at that date in the Dore valley just south of Dorstone. It is probable that they would also have been evident between Peterchurch and Bacton in the Golden Valley in the late 16th century. Over time people discovered how to use weirs to raise the level of water in rivers so that it could overflow to flood the land artificially to create 'water-meadows'.

Rowland's 'water-workes' incorporate both catchworks and bedworks. But in his scheme the bedwork was quite different from the much more common ridge-and-furrow systems used elsewhere in Britain, which it probably preceded. His approach involved a development of catchworks, in which water carried by channels from weirs and sluices diverting water from natural watercourses was distributed evenly over carefully levelled valley-bottom ground. Low ridges or terraces prevented the water from running away too quickly. Irrigation and drainage channels were developed to spread the water over the ground and create a shallow film which could then be drained in the spring to ensure early growth or flooded in the summer to irrigate in periods of drought.

The different elements in the system were illustrated in the 'Mapp of the Water-workes' (Map 4.2) found in the original edition of *His Booke* (not in the 1897 reprint, although referred to on p.108).

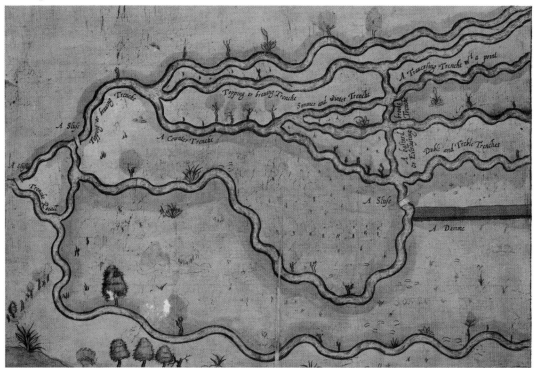

Map 4.2 Rowland's 'Mapp of the Water-workes' with the various types of trench labelled. (Courtesy of The Huntington Library, California, HM 69724)

43

The map shows an idealised layout for his system and he comments in *His Booke* that he named the different channels so that his workers could understand how the system worked. The principal channels identified in *His Booke* are interpreted below:

The *Trench Royal* was the main distributor and drainage channel running north-south more or less parallel to the river. In the southern section at Bacton it ran to the east of the river (Map 4.3), whereas the separate northern section lay west of the river between Peterchurch and Turnastone. The gap between Rowland's northern and southern waterworks arose because of his inability to convince the owner of Chanstone Court of the benefits of drowning. Rowland claimed his neighbour was losing £100 a year through not using drowning techniques.[9]

Topping or *Braving Trenches* were distribution channels about 1m wide and 0.5m deep, running within 2m of the river. They retained water for times when the river was low. The earth taken out of the trenches formed a bank as an additional protection against natural flooding. They were supplied by a series of sluices and weirs in the river at its upper end, and a series of dams or 'stankes' prevented all the water running away to lower ground. The dams may also refer to the use of terraces to break the gradient of the slope and check the flow of water.

Counter Trenches were probably distributor trenches which carried water from the river across the field and ensured that the thin film of water did not become stagnant and waterlog the field. They formed part of a hierarchy of trenches which crossed the field and became smaller as they formed a series of braided trenches to spread water through the use of 'summer and winter' trenches.

Summer and Winter Trenches were distributor trenches controlled by 'Bastard Sluices' on the Trench Royal and were used for summer and winter drowning, through controlled releases of water, but not run throughout the year. The term 'bastard' trench may refer to the practice in which the bottom of the trench had been subject to 'double digging' where a second spit was turned or removed from the base of the trench. The other distributor channels, which spread the water across the field, the counter trenches and the double and treble trenches, probably only had one spit removed.

Bastard Brook or *Everlasting Trench* carried water throughout the year and returned water from the Trench Royal to the river Dore. In this case the 'bastard' element probably refers to the diversion of the original course of the brook by digging an alternative channel.

Double and *Treble Trenches* were probably bedworks using parallel raised beds and drainage channels to form distribution networks across level ground in the valley floor.

A *Traversing Trench* was fed by a counter trench and water retained by the 'damme', probably relating to its function as an overflow channel. A *Damme* shown on his Plan probably refers to the large dam used to collect a head of water, and was one amongst a series of smaller *stankes*.

Rowland estimated that the Trench Royal 'can easily contain the inflow from brooks and springs along the way, and drown six score acres [120 acres] in 3 hours, and 20 acres in the return back. In a counter-trench 40 acres, in a traversing-trench, 20 more, in summer and winter trenches 20, in double and treble trenches 20 more. Take up the sluice that commands the stank-royal and in one hour my everlasting trench conveys the trench-royal and all its tributaries into the main river.'[10]

Rowland, through *His Booke* and in his 'water-workes' on the ground in the Golden Valley, was the first to document how the streams and topographical features of the Dore could be manipulated to create water-meadows. His schemes demonstrated how these systems could be constructed by adapting the pre-existing catchwork schemes to develop hybrid bedwork schemes more suitable to the different slopes and farming practices in the valley of the Dore. The detailed analysis of the purpose and operational relationships will be developed more fully in Chapter 6, but below are considered the main principles which Rowland developed for his first waterworks in the Newcourt/Bacton area. He states, 'Many have said to me, no other mans grounds lie so convenient to drowne as mine at Newcourt.'[11] It is significant that Rowland recognised that his system 'was not appropriate for major rivers like the Thames or the Severn, but scale of controlled flood with my trench system is perfectly achievable'.[12]

The Bacton-Newcourt waterworks

Rowland's original waterworks extended for about 2½ kilometres from where the Dore flows south of Chanstone Court, occupying lands forming part of his estate at Newcourt on the right bank of the river, with Morehampton lands on the left (east) side. The fall in the river over this stretch of the valley was from 100m above sea level below Chanstone to 90m where the Trench Royal joins the river Dore at Newcourt Mill. This fall of about 10 metres gave a very shallow gradient of 1:250. At its southern end below Newcourt, the river meandered in a very erratic way over this stretch of valley floor because of the low gradient and would have flooded easily. The Trench Royal may have been built to divert the flow from the Dore and even out its gradient to maintain a better flow with control of the timing and pattern of flooding on the adjacent fields.

The southern section of the Trench Royal starts south of Chanstone flowing on the east bank of the river. In doing so, over time the Trench Royal has captured the water from the river, and now appears to be the main watercourse. The straight lines of the canal have been modified by small meanders which have developed over time, so that at first sight the Trench Royal looks like a natural system. From Chanstone to Bacton the original Dore is little more than a tributary to the Trench Royal, its main use being to supply water to the now redundant Newcourt mill. Our field surveys have shown that since it was first dug the Trench Royal has worn down its bed to at least a metre below the level of the river bed where the two separate, so that this part of the river is dry in its upper reaches. When the Trench Royal was originally dug the series of straight line channels would have gained height relative to the river until water from the canal could flood the fields between it and the river Dore, and then drain back into the river. This section of Rowland's waterworks was probably started in 1584-5, shortly after he moved to Newcourt with his first wife Elizabeth, and developed over a number of years subsequently.

Rowland had another trench dug linking the Trench Royal and the River Dore, north of his house at Newcourt, which was both a feeder canal to the waterworks on his side of the river, and to the mill-leat. It supplied water to drown the fields between Newcourt and the river, as well as to power Newcourt mill. Rowland wrote: 'My Mill is my first Worke, governed by a little Bastard-Brooke, fedde with eight living Springs.' It is hard to count the springs today, because it is clear that watercourses which ran in Rowland's day are now dry. The aerial photograph (Fig. 4.3) shows that the channel/mill-leat can still be traced, as well as gullies leading into it down which water must once have flowed.

Rowland claimed that his Trench Royal could be made to flow both ways, which sounds as though he was claiming (as usual) to be able to do the impossible. However, assuming that the Trench on the Newcourt side of the river was dead level, gaining height above the descending river, and was fed by springs along its length, this is entirely possible. By closing a sluice at one end or the other, water in the trench could have been made to flow either way.

In *His Booke* he describes a 'Stank Royal' – a major earth bank, which held back the water before it flowed into territory beyond his control at Bacton at the downstream end of his waterworks. The southern part of the meadows has a water channel running south which runs parallel to the mill tail but does not drain back to the river Dore (Fig. 4.2).

He writes a dramatic description of himself standing on this bank during a violent storm, exulting over his works. 'Take heed the water exceed not the height of any of your stanks or damms a hayrs-breadth; for the force of the water and violence of the winde in a furious tempest, will over-throw it, as if the Canon plaid against it. I have forborne to speake of my Stank-Royall, which is of purpose prepared to intertaine the Trench-royall which ... in his running, undertakes the safe conduct of three brookes and some Springes ...'.[13] Little, if anything, can be seen of the bank today, although a sketch-map drawn by the late Colin Davies of Maentwlch Farm shows a long three-to-four-foot high bank parallel to the river just upstream of where it flows under the road bridge at Bacton. Colin remembered the bank from his boyhood in the 1930s.

The waterworks on this part of the system appear to have all been contained between the Trench Royal to the east of the river and the channel/leat on the west side. However, LIDAR images show workings further east, where spring-fed gullies come down from the hills, which could be interpreted as having been part of the scheme. Rather mysteriously, the water-filled Trench Royal returns to the river close to Newcourt, although its line continues without trace of a trench until it starts to re-appear and to accumulate water further downstream.

The lack of distinct features may be due to the smaller areas of meadowland between the Trench Royal and the Dore in this part of the valley and the proximity of the 'park pale' which enclosed the Newcourt deer park. Rowland states in his book 'my park pale came within twenty foot of my Trench Royall', which must have further restricted the building of trenches, especially as Morehampton had a park pale almost opposite Newcourt (see Map 4.3). The 'eye of the believer' may be required to find visual evidence at ground level, but there are visible signs

Fig. 4.2 Drainage channel at southern end of Newcourt/Bacton water-meadows

of earthworks available on aerial photographs and from LIDAR scans, and land use/field-name evidence from the 1842 tithe maps suggests more extensive areas of meadowland (see Map 4.4).

Map 4.3 distinguishes the Trench Royal (purple) from the river Dore (blue). Its course to the east of the river enclosed an area which could be managed as water-meadows. There is very little evidence today of remnants of carriers or drainage channels in this area, but the Trench Royal is linked to the river by two trenches which carried water from the Trench Royal westward to the Dore (in red). To the east of the Trench Royal, Morehampton Park farm has several water features dating from the period, including a moat, fish-ponds and drainage

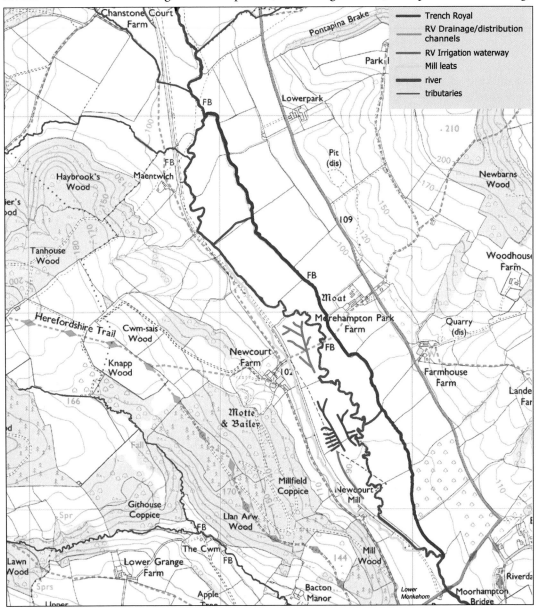

Map 4.3 *Rowland's southern waterworks at Newcourt/Bacton.*
(© *Crown copyright 2016 OS Licence No.100057492*)

channels. However, the slope is towards the Trench Royal and is only fed by one stream so that any waterworks would have been restricted to the lower slopes. The area has also been intensively farmed and few traces remain.

From the aerial photograph (see Map 3.6) it is evident that the area around Newcourt/Bacton today is characterised by permanent pasture in the south and arable in the north. However, the 1842 tithe map of land use at that time (Map 4.4) shows a very different picture.

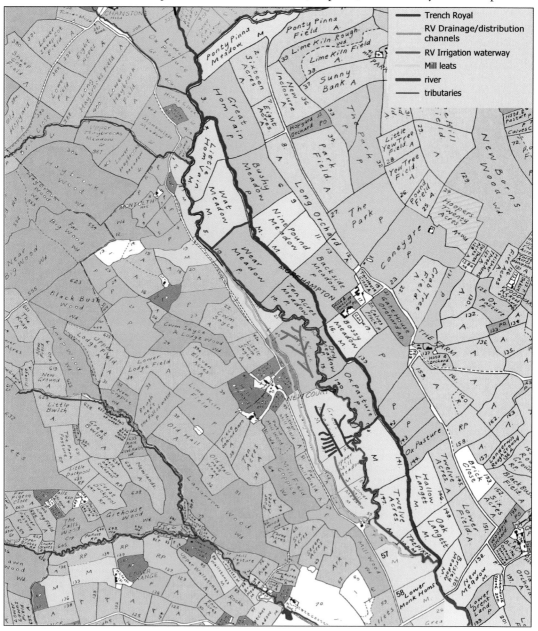

Map 4.4 Rowland Vaughan's use of water overlaid on 1842-43 tithe map – Newcourt/Bacton area. (For key to land use colour coding see Map 3.7)

In this map, the field names are revealing – the two arable fields between the river Dore and the Trench Royal in the north of the area were called 'Wet Meadow' and 'Weir Meadow' in the tithe map. The middle section has reverted to pasture but the field with remnants of Rowland's drainage channels was called 'Dry Meadow' and 'Cow Pasture'.

The area south of Newcourt, which still has remnants of irrigation channels between the mill leat and the river Dore, and the Dore and the Trench Royal, also showed extensive evidence of water-meadows in place names – e.g. 'Great Meadow' – and in land use. The links with the

Fig. 4.3 Remnants of water features at Newcourt (aerial photo taken in 2014). The curving line of the mill leat can be seen to the right of the farm track (which is the track bed of the former railway). The winding tree-lined feature at the bottom is the original course of the river Dore.

(a)

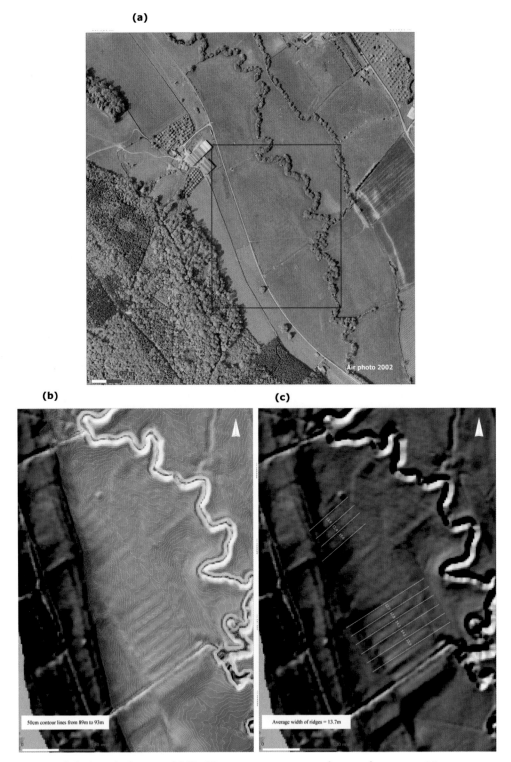

Air photo 2002

(b)

50cm contour lines from 89m to 93m

(c)

Average width of ridges = 13.7m

*Fig. 4.4 Aerial photo and LIDAR images: remnants of water features at Newcourt;
possible bedworks.*

watermill are evident in the place names 'Upper' and 'Lower Mill Meadows'. The area east of the Trench Royal also has evidence of water management using the Trench Royal to create meadows such as 'Bushy Meadow', 'Nine Pound Meadow', 'Backside Meadow' and 'Bossy Meadow' around Morehampton Park farm.

Rowland's schemes always used more than one natural water source to ensure a water supply throughout the year. In *His Booke* he comments on a scheme in Shropshire where the water supplies were insufficient 'And so I assure you that you will find many lands neglected and giving a poor return, for lack of proper water management. With proper application of my system it is possible to graze the meadows up till May, and still have two mowings per year, giving a substantial financial return. A Mr Hoord of Shropshire attempted to follow a similar system, but his mistake was not selecting lands with a good supply of winter and summer water for the drowning system.'[14]

Evidence for the development of water-meadows in the Newcourt area is concentrated to the west of the river Dore and east of the mill leat (shown in yellow on Map 4.3), which is fed by streams flowing off the adjacent uplands and by water diverted by a weir off the Dore. The mill leat flows for about 1 kilometre and the mill tail returns to the Dore just before the Dore is joined by the Trench Royal. The map also indicates that the area between the mill leat and the river Dore has evidence which indicates remnants of possible 'hybrid bedworks' with irrigation channels (shown in red/orange on Map 4.3) that drained back to the Dore. An area just north of these meadows has an extensive pattern of drainage channels (shown in orange) which could have originated as part of Rowland's scheme, but also demonstrate straighter lines more characteristic of later agricultural drainage.

The aerial photograph and LIDAR images of the Newcourt area (Figs. 4.3 & 4.4) show the remnants of Rowland's original water management system such as the mill leat and drainage channels. The water used to spread over these fields was controlled by sluices and weirs on the Trench Royal where the linking channels (shown in red on Map 4.4) flow between the Trench Royal and the Dore.

At the northern end, water was diverted into the Dore. This flooded the meadows between the mill leat and the Dore, and these were drained by the extensive pattern of drainage channels. This area shows evidence of possible bedworks opposite Newcourt with two areas having bedworks which drain back to the Dore (see Fig. 4.4). These images show how the contours fall from west to east from 93 to 89 metres. The bedworks are clearly evident in the LIDAR image with an average width of 13.7m, which is significantly larger than the average of 3-11m for traditional ridge and furrow in the Golden Valley, identified earlier in Map 3.1.

The meadow called Monkehom

Rowland was a persistent purchaser of and dealer in property. As early as 1583 he and his brother-in-law Robert Knollys had attempted to recover the extensive Brecon estates of Sir Roger Vaughan of Porthaml and in 1595 he became locked in an argument with John Parry of Poston over his lease of Snodhill Park in Peterchurch. In that same year he was also in dispute with John Parry of Morehampton over an acre or two of meadow in Bacton called 'Monkehom'. Of these three cases the family disagreement over the small field in Bacton seems the most trivial, yet Rowland went to considerable trouble to settle the matter.[15] In the context of his waterworks it is of special interest.

Land issues in the Golden Valley became more complicated following Henry VIII's seizure of the monasteries, when up to one-third of all landed property in England was put on the market. In the valley the little river Dore divided Dore Abbey's grange (or sheep farm) of Morehampton on the east bank from the manor of Newcourt on the west. In the last years of the abbey, Morehampton grange, including the pasture of 'Monkehom' (which was on the west bank of the river), was held on a long lease by Thomas Baskerville,[16] who farmed it in the traditional manner as a sheep farm. The field, or part of it, once pasture belonging to Dore Abbey, can be identified on the 1842 Bacton tithe map bordering the river Dore (see Map 4.4, bottom right).[17] When, following the dissolution of the abbey in 1537, Henry VIII granted the grange to Stephen Parry and his wife Jane, they leased it to Sir Roger Vaughan. The Parrys and Baskervilles were related by marriage and the grazing on 'Monkehom', not without dispute on occasion, passed from one to another, with Stephen Parry converting its use, in accordance with changing husbandry, to pasture for his cattle and plough oxen and as a stopover for Welsh cattle being driven by stages to London. For convenience, they erected a simple farm bridge over the Dore and in about 1543 Stephen Parry built a watermill for Morehampton.

The mill created trouble. Firstly, it was built partly on 'Monkehom' field. Secondly, after her husband's death Jane Parry added floodgates and had a trench dug to take away the surplus water running down the pasture. Thirdly, she then leased the greater part of the now divided pasture to Newcourt. Then, fourthly, the bridge was carried away in a flood and rebuilt below the mill. By the time of the next generation, when Rowland was at Newcourt and John Parry at Morehampton, the division and ownership of 'Monkehom', renamed by Rowland as *Porva ir Gwartheg* (Welsh for 'grass for cattle' or 'Cow Pasture'), was thoroughly muddled and dependent upon the memories of a dozen and more 60- and 70-year-old witnesses. Lastly, the mill introduced an additional trench, the mill leat, unconnected with Rowland's *water-workes*, across the small area which from today's aerial photography is riddled with landmarks (see Map 4.3). These include the leats on both sides of the river Dore for the Newcourt and Morehampton watermills, Rowland's Trench Royal and the track bed of the disused late 19th-century Golden Valley railway which destroyed the original course of the river.

The importance of 'Monkehom' to Rowland was its position in the very area suited for the final downstream dam of his *water-workes*, which remained within living memory. Many questions arise. There is no hint in the evidence of the elderly local witnesses that the new trench was, or had been, anything more than a mill-leat. Moreover they made no mention of other pre-dissolution trenches nor of excavations in progress in or near 'Monkehom'. It would appear, therefore, from the written evidence that in 1595 Rowland's work had not yet reached that area, but allowing for the usual legal delays the dispute could have been simmering for some time. The date of the start of surveying, levelling and beginning work on the trenches is arguable. By his own account he began before his first wife Elizabeth's death but was delayed by local opposition. The legal record also casts doubt on Rowland's delightful tale of his curiosity aroused by a flooded molehill: 'In the month of March ... I happened to finde a mole or wants nest, raised on the brim of the brooke, like a great hillocke; from which nest or hillocke, there issued a little streame of water, drawne by the working of the wante downe a shelving or descending ground ... The running of which little streame did wonderfully content mee, seeing it pleasing greene ... This was the first cause I undertook the drowning of grounds.'[18] Was he in fact inspired by the trenches dug for the Morehampton mill?

If settlement of these three disputes were of direct importance to Rowland there is no such explanation for his decision, also in 1595, to buy the *Craswall Dayeries* from William Herbert of Oldcastle for the considerable sum of £600. Oldcastle is below the southern end of Hatterell Hill on the Black Mountains and the *Dayeries*, (a 16th-century 'dairy farm'), were probably the large open pastures around the ruins of Craswall Priory. Both were well over 12 remote kilometres away and unconnected with Newcourt. At a similar distance he was by 1601 in possession of rights in the manor of Howton, near Pontrilas at the foot of the Golden Valley, a more explicable acquisition because the manor boundary ran down to the river Dore and later became the site of a forge established by the Baskervilles.[19] Six years later he disposed of Howton, perhaps in order to reinvest elsewhere. With partners he dabbled in land at Tremorithic in Bacton and in some newly enclosed land in Dorstone, but far more importantly he aimed to extend his waterworks well beyond the Newcourt estate.[20] Despite debts it was in 1607 that he made his two most momentous acquisitions.

In 1607, Rowland was granted a 21-year lease by Sir James Scudamore over the Dore Abbey lands and watermill, which his father had bought from the Crown in 1545 after the dissolution of the monasteries. He held this lease for 16 years.

One of these could have been in his mind for some time. John Scudamore, the Crown Receiver for Dore Abbey at its dissolution in 1537, had in 1545 bought the whole site of the abbey and surrounding lands from the Crown. His great-grandson, Sir James Scudamore of Holme Lacy, agreed in 1607 to lease to Rowland the abbots' former lodging, with other houses and buildings, including the water mill within the precincts, and all the demesne lands, pasture and meadows, for 21 years. The rent of £200 a year was considerable, but Rowland grabbed at the deal. Although he may have been doing nothing more than taking the opportunity to enlarge his estate by adding these lands adjoining Newcourt, he must surely also have been musing on the possibilities of stretching his waterworks across the abbey's meadows.[21] Nowhere, however, is there any mention of irrigation works on the old abbey's lands either in 1607 or during the following 16 years of Rowland's tenancy.

In that same year of 1607 he made a second significant purchase by obtaining from John Parry of Poston rights in a range of property extending across the parishes of Turnastone and Vowchurch including three houses, land, the advowson, parsonage, glebe and tithes of Turnastone parish, and sheep pastures high on the Turnastone hillside. It cost him £310, but the deal allowed him to stretch his waterworks through the meadows beyond Newcourt to most of the ten further kilometres to Peterchurch, with the exception of Chanstone Court farm lands in Vowchurch.[22] The three unnamed houses and church tithes brought income but possibly also some opposition to his waterworks from the tenants. More gratifying, the advowson (the right to appoint the parish parson) gave him a desirable symbol of rank.

The purchase was balanced the following year by assigning the advowson of Peterchurch to Thomas Morgan of Blackmoor in Abbeydore. Eventually, in 1615 John Parry of Poston, then living in London as Controller of the King's Household, recovered his Peterchurch estates from Rowland, Morgan and others who had been using them for underwriting other loans and settlements. These included the valuable Peterchurch tithes, woodland within Snodhill Park and houses on the fringe of Peterchurch village at Wellbrook. Specifically excluded were 'one watercourse running and being in the close called Monks Close with free egress and regress to the same' and seven acres adjoining the river Dore.[23] 'Monks Close' was beside the river and church in Peterchurch whilst the seven-acre field on the parish boundary, later named 'Weir Meadow', was at the point where the Trenant brook feeds into the Dore at the highest point of Rowland's Trench Royal. Both were essential for the waterworks.

The complexity of Rowland's scheme as he extended it to the northern section of the Dore and the influence of the natural environment on the development of water management systems will be examined in more detail in Chapter 6, 'The Drowning of the Valley'.

5   THE ENTERPRISING SQUIRE

Although Rowland is best known for his scheme of 'water-workes', he was also energetically making efforts, in the early years after his marriage, to raise his status and wealth in other ways. As a second son and despite the support he received from his family, he had to depend upon his own resources, in which marriage took an important place. Indeed, throughout his life family marriages influenced Rowland's fortunes and misfortunes. As with so many aspects of his life, the facts available are confusing and occasionally questionable. Even the legal evidence produced in lawsuits, sometimes reciting events of 10 or 20 years earlier, may be suspect. Successive modern authors writing about Rowland have been misled by conflicting sources or have traced only part of the story.[1]

However, from the date of his first marriage it is quite clear that Rowland would not be content with the life of a country landowner. Designing and experimenting with his novel scheme for drowning the meadows at Newcourt would fill his mind and occupy his time for the next 20 years. Even so, it did not exhaust his energy and ambitions: in the same period he was coming forward with other ideas and suggestions, though finding it difficult to have his voice heard.

His domestic activity was limited to the seasonal hunting in the deer park. Consequently, after England went to war against Spain in 1585 and the call came from Henry, earl of Pembroke, to serve as a captain of the militia in Hereford city and the west Herefordshire hundreds of Webtree and Ewyas Lacy during the threat of the Spanish invasion in 1588, it was a welcome relief.[2] He wrote proudly of: 'Being one of hir Maiesties Captaines, raised in eighty-eight',[3] a threat averted when the Spanish Armada was defeated by a combination of naval battle and severe weather. As a member of the local gentry he had also evidently been appointed a Justice of the Peace, or magistrate, as it would have been in that capacity that in the following year he joined the jury of the Commission of Sewers of the river Wye. On such occasions he would, as in London, have regularly worn a gentleman's tall hat and carried a sword.[4] In *His Booke* he reveals his knowledge of local affairs and his frustration with their protective management by the powerful landowners. Nevertheless, he was typically bold enough to appeal directly to one of the most influential men at Court and in south Wales and the Marches to assist his solutions for reform.

An Act of Parliament of 1531 had introduced the appointment of local Commissions of Sewers, judicial bodies with juries, to oversee the drainage of rivers and the prevention of their flooding. The Commission appointed for the river Wye in 1588-89 was faced with not only the seasonal flooding of riverside meadows, but also competing interests: firstly of the mill-owners, of which the industrial mills at Hereford belonging to the dean and chapter of the cathedral and at Monmouth belonging to the Crown had the largest weirs; secondly of the riparian landowners with their salmon fisheries; and thirdly of the boatmen consequently blocked from taking their barges and trows upriver. The Commissioners were similarly divided between the grandee landowners, amongst whom William Herbert, Lord Pembroke, represented the Crown's interest in the great Monmouth weirs, and the hauliers who were obliged to take heavy goods on Herefordshire's notoriously bad roads.

Rowland favoured the improvement of the navigation but could make no headway against the immmoveable landowners defending their right to keep the profitable salmon weirs. They would have regarded him as an interfering young troublemaker. He was in fact not an entirely objective spokesman on behalf of the traders on the river, who brought coal and wine upstream from Bristol and the Forest of Dean, and exported timber and bark downstream, for he was personally interested in the traffic between the Golden Valley and the Forest of Dean. He would have been fully aware that the second Lord Pembroke was the Constable of the Forest at the time when the Commission ordered the destruction of weirs, only to be frustrated in 1589 when the city of Hereford was successful in persuading the Privy Council to overrule the Commissioners to the benefit of the city mills, protected by the Hereford Mills Act of 1555. In *His Booke* (1610) he delicately laid the matter before his patron, the third Lord Pembroke, who two years before had been appointed Constable of the Forest and consequently wielded powerful influence. However, nothing was changed then, nor in 1622 when another Commission, on which Rowland almost certainly did not sit, again attempted to have the weirs removed, without success.[5]

In the 16th century the Royal Forest of Dean was one of the country's age-old centres of iron-works. Industry was moving out of the medieval cities like Hereford with their restrictive guilds hampering the enlargement of new industries, particularly those dependent on water power. In the mid-century the traditional bloom furnaces in the Forest, 20 miles south of the Golden Valley, were being replaced by more powerful blast furnaces on the fast-flowing streams running into the Wye between Symonds Yat and Tintern. Rowland would, as a Wye Commissioner, have known about the expansion of the new forges and furnaces on both sides of the river and the profits being made by the few leading landowners with licence from the Crown to extract iron and set up furnaces within the Forest, of whom the biggest were Wintour of Lydney and Lord Pembroke. They faced great handicap, though, in the form of fees and limitations imposed by the Crown for felling the timber to provide charcoal for the furnaces. Despite its distance from the nearest source of the iron ore and the difficulties of transporting it overland, the one advantage the Golden Valley could offer was an abundance of timber to fire forges unrestricted by the laws of the royal forest. Later in the century the accounts of the west Herefordshire forges show that charcoal from Peterchurch was considerably cheaper than elsewhere.[6]

Rowland, indeed, had a growing interest in the use and power of water. In the 1580s he was already experimenting with irrigating the water-meadows at Bacton. His appointment to the Commission of Sewers of the Wye in 1588-89 would have shown him not only the potential for harnessing the river Dore a few miles further upstream to power the first forge in west Herefordshire but also the possibility of using the Wye for transport if it could be made navigable. He even mentioned on the last page of *His Booke* the use of water power for turning roasting spits and powering a sawmill, writing: 'Those that are desirous to see a Mill sawing Timber, there shall their desires bee fully satisfied, seeing a Mill by a Water-course, keepe a dozen Sawes on worke together.'[7] Influenced therefore by his knowledge of ironworking in the Forest of Dean, the blast furnace for glass-making built by 1580 at St Weonards, between the Golden Valley and Monmouth, and possibly also by the Bringewood forge at work in 1584 near Ludlow, Rowland could see the possibilities of starting another scheme more instantly profitable than the irrigation of the Bacton water-meadows.[8] By coincidence, in the early 1590s he had an opportunity to act, and this time he obtained partners – his brother Henry Vaughan of Moccas and James Baskerville of Pontrilas.

In the days before banking, loans had to be obtained either from professional money-lenders or through the support of wealthy relations and neighbours. The success of the system depended, as Rowland was himself to experience, upon good will and honest behaviour.[9] In 1593 a desperate call for help had come from his cousin James Parry of Poston, held as a debtor in the Fleet prison in London with unpaid debts to city moneylenders. James Parry's estate in the Golden Valley sprawled across Vowchurch, Turnastone, Peterchurch and Snodhill. His freedom and property were at risk if he did not settle the debts and he begged Rowland to pay them for him, offering in return the income from the Peterchurch tithes for some years. Rowland seized his chance. He pressed James Parry and his two sons to give him also the use of Snodhill Park until the loan would be cleared in three years' time. Parry negotiated the right to retain the minerals of gold, silver, tin and lead and doubtless thought he had made a satisfactory bargain. But he had fallen into the trap. Rowland was not interested in unknown and probably non-existent minerals. He was after the 1,200 good timber trees in the park.[10]

The partners quickly ran into trouble for in 1596 James Parry took them to court for felling the timber, to which Rowland responded that only the minerals had been excepted. Although the outcome of the lawsuit in the Star Chamber has not been traced, it would appear that some compromise was reached, for the two families continued their land deals and the forge survived. Other forges were set up in west Herefordshire, including one before 1623 at nearby Pontrilas by the Baskervilles, all later passing into the iron-manufacturing empire of the Foleys of Stoke Edith. Peterchurch forge was still active in 1705 but was not in production in 1736 and apparently closed before 1750. The mill-pond was grassland by 1843 but the cottage became a blacksmith's shop and ultimately the late 16th-century stone and timber-framed house was destroyed in a fire in the 1970s. Its site opposite the Nag's Head inn was ploughed out in 1983

north elevation   *south elevation*

Fig. 5.1 Sketch elevation of Peterchurch Forge from RCHME 1931.
(Reproduced by permission of Historic England)

Fig. 5.2 Photograph of Peterchurch Forge from RCHME 1931.
(Reproduced by permission of Historic England)

but pieces of slag and the patch of dark soil marking the charcoal waste can still be found as marks of Rowland's pioneering forge.[11]

Up to this point Rowland's enterprises had been limited to those for which he could obtain support from the family. He still, however, hankered to obtain an appointment in the service of the Crown. Even though he considered her support had been inconsistent, with the death of Blanche Parry in 1590 he lacked any direct contact with the royal Court. He therefore tried to attract the queen's notice himself. According to his own, perhaps biased, account to William Cecil of Allt yr Ynys, Lord Burghley's cousin, the queen was polite and thought him very suitable.[12] Nevertheless, no appointment resulted. By 1597 he was seeking other channels. He appealed in person to William Cecil to contact Lord Burghley's son, Sir Robert Cecil. Sir Robert was now in charge of administration for his father, who would die the following year. William Cecil's 1597 letter shows that Rowland was not his priority either but something of an afterthought. 'I forgot to crave your honour to prefer this bearer [Rowland Vaughan] to be one of Her Majesty's Guard, there being divers wanting, and he being a sufficient man for that place. And Her Majesty, lately taking the air in Islington Fields, noted this bearer then there being a shooting, and of her goodness said he was a feat man to attend her service.'[13] Rowland himself took this letter to Sir Robert Cecil but no appointment resulted. Still seeking a patron, in 1601 he was probably the 'Mr. Vaughan of Herefordshire' who offered his services at the time of the rebellion of the earl of Essex. His offer was ignored.

At this point he decided to draw on what he claimed as his own experiences. He had knowledge of local affairs but when he attempted to bring about change, be it concerning the mills and navigation of the Wye, agricultural improvement, or care of the poor, he was frustrated.

He lacked both personal influence and a powerful patron. He therefore turned to the age-old patron of the Vaughans, the Herbert family. Their ancient centres of power still lay in south Wales and the Marches where for generations the Vaughan and Parry families had been their loyal followers. Moreover, Rowland had some slight personal contact with them in connection with the Wye valley mines, salmon weirs and navigation.

William Herbert, 3rd earl of Pembroke succeeded his father in 1601. He had been a popular favourite in Queen Elizabeth I's Court until his mistress Mary Fitton (who it has been suggested was the 'dark lady' of Shakespeare's sonnets) became pregnant. In February 1601 both were banished from Court and Lord Herbert spent time in the Fleet prison. He recovered his position by racing to Edinburgh on the news of the queen's death in 1603 to ingratiate himself with James VI of Scotland, now also James I of England. The two men became close friends and the king frequently stayed with Lord Herbert at his English country home of Wilton House in Wiltshire. Lord Herbert was an outstanding patron of the arts and with his brother was probably the dedicatee for the First Folio of Shakespeare's plays. He gave his name to Pembroke College, Oxford and, having invested in Bermuda, Pembroke Parish there is also named after him. His patronage was commercially useful, hence Rowland's flowery address and panegyrics in introducing *His Booke*. In addition, Rowland cannily began indirectly by not writing about the water-meadows but by first raising other matters to attract Lord Herbert's attention. The most arresting of these was the national concern for the alarming rise in the number of paupers and vagrants. In 1601 the Poor Law Act had been passed and by 1604 Rowland was preparing *His Booke* describing his innovative waterworks, so it was a good moment to approach the new earl.

In Queen Elizabeth I's reign poverty was a major problem. The population of England had at last recovered from the devastation of the Black Death two hundred years earlier, and was continuing to increase. Over the same period the amount of land under the plough, not required for that smaller population, had been significantly reduced by the spread of enclosure and pasturage. Open fields still remained in parts of the Golden Valley but Rowland's own enclosures in 1605 and the extension of his meadows in Vowchurch and Peterchurch, including the meadow in Vowchurch between the bridge and tithe barn opposite the church, contributed to the shortage of cultivated land now needed for a growing population.[14] Emigration to the towns followed, but locally Hereford's earlier cloth-making industry had ceased and the city was in decline.

Periodic poor harvests across the country including Herefordshire at the end of the 16th century, especially in 1586-87 and the later 1590s, led to a serious growth of poverty. This inevitably caused rioting, epidemics and outbreaks of the dreaded plague. In and about Herefordshire there were high mortality rates in 1597 and 1607. Faced with the increasing numbers of the poor and the growth of vagrancy and unruly behaviour, the government introduced acts of Parliament to control vagrants and provide care for the poor. Of these, the most important was the Poor Law of 1601, which remained the basis for the parochial treatment of poverty under the supervision of the magistrates for the next two centuries.[15]

Rowland was therefore familiar with the situation. He claimed in *His Booke* that 'There bee within a mile and a halfe from my house [Newcourt] every way, five hundred poore habitations; whose greatest meanes consist in spinning Flaxe, Hempe, and Hurdes [tow, the coarser part of flax and hemp]',[16] combined with begging, gleaning and scrumping. He was exaggerating. There were and still are few houses within a mile and a half of Newcourt and even by stretching the radius to two miles it only contains all of Bacton and parts of Turnastone, Vowchurch, Newton St Margaret's, and Abbeydore. Nevertheless, scrolling forward 50 years, both the Militia Assessments of 1663 and the Hearth Tax of 1664 indicate that the area between the Golden Valley and the Welsh border had fewer large estates and greater poverty than other parts of Herefordshire. In 1664, in the whole of the five parishes above there were 126 houses that were exempt from paying the tax plus a further 74 with only a single hearth, making a total of 200 small cottages likely to have been inhabited by the poor. Even that number is surprisingly large for this rural area of scattered houses where the spread of cottages on the local commons at Ewyas Harold and Vowchurch did not begin until a century later. This comparison usefully serves as a warning that both in *His Booke* and in giving evidence in lawsuits Rowland's figures, whether of numbers of people, sums of money or lengths of years, need to be treated with caution.

Rowland was unfolding a vision.[17] He had already built an additional watermill at Bacton, or reconstructed the existing overshot watermill. Perhaps having in mind his great-aunt Blanche Parry's intention to leave money for a parish almshouse and knowing of the many Tudor benefactions elsewhere for new hospitals, colleges and schools, he was led to contemplate the foundation of his Commonwealth. In doing so he was two or three centuries ahead of his time but he lacked the wealth of 19th-century benefactors to build a community like Saltaire or Port Sunlight in the Golden Valley. Instead he looked to Lord Pembroke and others for patronage and donations. *His Booke* was a prospectus, putting forward desirable schemes, in this case the complex of buildings, occupants and trades of an idealistic 'Commonwealth'.

He envisaged a community with housing, workshops, bedrooms, chimneys and 'cisterns' (both, at that time, luxuries in a cottage) for his 2,000 experienced craftsmen and workers of every trade: clothiers operating 20 broad looms and 10 narrow looms, brewers and bakers, carpenters, tanners and launderers, glovers, smiths, gardeners, lantern-makers and many others.[18] A cottage industry of some 200 non-resident poor spinners and carders would supply the cloth-mill. There would be a communal dining room, kitchen and stores, slaughter-house, brewery and cellar, a furnace and ovens. The whole operation would be under the eye of a clerk, imposing fixed prices and undertaking the marketing of the manufactured goods. There would be a chapel with a preacher paid a generous £50 a year for giving sermons, which would be compulsory to attend.

Rowland, or his scrivener, went so far as to draw a bird's-eye view of this imaginary collegiate settlement on a rustic site similar to but more spacious than Newcourt (Fig. 5.3). At bottom right is a prominent large quadrangle of '50 tenements for artificers', with the almshouses to the right, and the chapel nearby on the left. Above that is the slaughter-house with a separate office building. Adjacent is the mill-house (with water wheel) and the brew-house. At top right are extensive formal gardens and neatly arranged shrubs, fruit bushes perhaps, leading down to a strong river running horizontally across the page. A range of buildings on the left of the garden includes the kitchen (with a plume of dark smoke pouring out), larder, pantry and buttery, all serving the principal house. The house is a crenellated building built over the mill leat, with a cross-wing where Rowland saw himself presiding in the wainscotted dining room, over not only his workmen but a regular stream of guests and patrons, entertained in front of

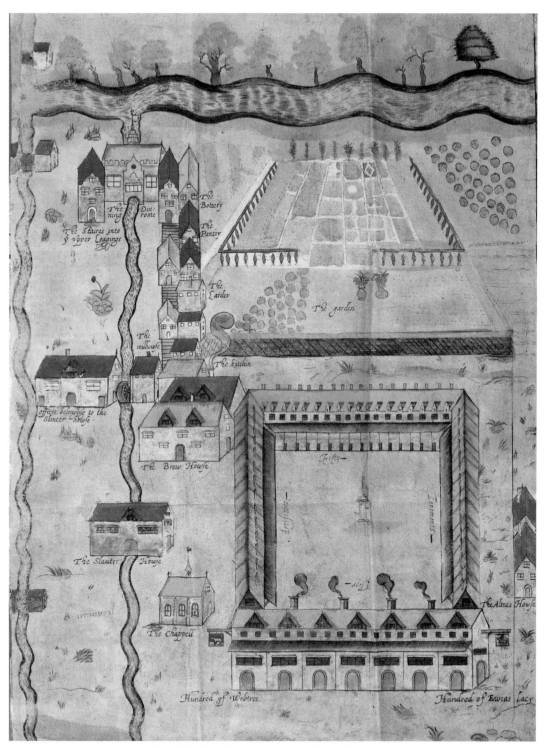

Fig. 5.3 The Commonwealth from His Booke.
(Courtesy of The Huntington Library, California, HM 69724)

a roaring fire by 'all sortes of Musicke plaies' and plied with meats and venison pasties from his park.[19] An upstairs lodging house is to the left, and then, served by separate leats, two further water wheels.

Rowland openly admitted that he had a personal stake in the whole ambitious plan, boasting that his estate with its 600 cattle, 3,000 sheep, 10 plough-lands, four mills, timber, stone and bricks ('Your Lordship sees I am force'd to doe, and over-doe, as one that must doe All, else nothing will bee done') would supply the Commonwealth with all its needs to his benefit.[20] However, it was impractical. He readily recognised that he did not have the financial resources to put it into effect. Looked at objectively the impressive numbers of his contacts and potential supporters among the nobles, judiciary, episcopate and gentry were unlikely to contribute to a scheme for the benefit of a remote local community in the Welsh Marches. Nor did the scheme meet the philanthropic aim of helping the poor and unemployed because he was looking only for skilled tradesmen. As in an army barracks, untrained apprentices, women and children were not wanted.

His Booke opens with a 13-page 'panegyrecke' by John Davies of Hereford, a lengthy poem extolling the wonders of Rowland's waterworks and his commonwealth. John Davies of Hereford (*c*.1565-1618), a close friend of Rowland, was a writing-master and an Anglo-Welsh poet. He wrote copiously on theological and philosophical themes as well as composing many epigrams on his contemporaries. The panegyric is followed by nine shorter poems in praise of the waterworks, the other authors being little-known apart from John Hoskins, sergeant at law, who was of a local family but moved in influential London circles and was elected MP for Hereford in 1604. Next follows the dedication to The Rt Hon. William, earl of Pembroke, Lord Herbert of Cardiff etc. (1580-1630), thus seeking publicity by benefiting from the tradition of family patronage.

Rowland, meanwhile, had tired of the idea of his commonwealth. He ended this opening part of *His Booke* with the words 'I have done with my Mechanicals, and the hopefull river of Wye; only I will fixe this accidentall merryment in the frontispiece (or broad-brow) of my Preface to my Water-workes,' and moved on to other matters.[21]

Before doing likewise, we must catch up with his domestic affairs which, at the beginning of this chapter, had left Rowland mourning the early death of his wife Elizabeth in about 1587 but still living with his sons at Newcourt. Under the law of 'English Courtesy' a widower was allowed to remain in occupation of the family home for his lifetime. According to the documents Rowland continued to do so until 1612, a date that fits what little is known of his second wife, Anne Jones. She, like his first wife, came into Rowland's life bringing him an inheritance of a home, but an even finer one.

Anne was the granddaughter of Symond Parry. Symond (Simon) Parry (died 1573), brother of Milo, was lord both of the manor of Bacton and of Jenkyn ap Richard (now part of Newton St Margaret's) together with its newly-built house, which he described in his will as his 'mansion' of Whitehouse. Symond Parry's will was proved by Griffith Jones (died 1578) of Llowes, across the Wye in Radnorshire, who had married Symond's elder daughter Jane. A younger daughter, Maud, married John Berrowe, whose family will enter Rowland's life later. Griffith and Jane Jones also had two daughters (see the pedigree chart on p.12).[22] The elder, Anne, who inherited Whitehouse on her father's death in 1578, married Rowland *c*.1593-95. Thus for a second time

Fig. 5.4 The Elizabethan wing of Whitehouse, Vowchurch

Rowland made a marriage with a grand house attached. Anne's younger sister Blanche, who if she outlived both Anne and Rowland would inherit Whitehouse, married Epiphan Howorth in 1590. Howorth became one of the central figures in Rowland's later years. Of a gentry family, his grandfather had come from the north of England to Herefordshire where the family had settled at Prior's Court at Widemarsh Moor in Hereford. Following his marriage to Blanche Jones he entered into Rowland's circle and named his eldest son Rowland (Howorth).

While his marriage to Anne brought Rowland another estate, it also embroiled him and his new brother-in-law in at least two legal disputes in which they acted together. The first, in 1595, probably of only peripheral concern to Rowland, was an argument about leases of lands in Radnorshire made by Griffith Jones shortly before his death.[23] The second was closer to home. Jane Jones, the widowed mother of Anne and Blanche, had married a certain Robert Vaughan and when she was dying in 1597 she asked Robert to divide all her goods at Whitehouse, including plate, money and jewels worth £200, between her daughters. Robert agreed but had done nothing about it when he fell ill two years later, only a few months after marrying a widow named Elizabeth. When it became clear that he was dying, swift action had to be taken to protect the girls' interests and prevent Elizabeth from gaining administration of everything at Whitehouse. Rowland's son William[24] arrived from Newcourt just in time to see Robert's will made and to be named as one of the executors, and on the following day Epiphan used a mixture of threats and bribery to persuade Elizabeth to sign everything over to him. He and Rowland then divided the property according to Jane's wishes, leaving Elizabeth no recourse other than to bring an unsuccessful Chancery case against them.[25]

This period was the peak of Rowland's life as an enterprising country gentleman. He had again married well. Anne bore him another son, Richard, and two daughters, Elizabeth and Katherine.[26] When later Rowland was spending much of his time in London, Anne brought

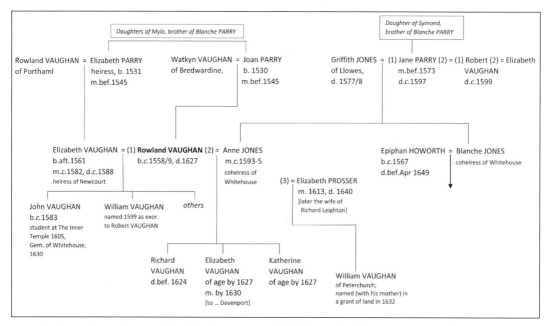

Pedigree chart showing the following content:

Daughters of Mylo, brother of Blanche PARRY

Daughter of Symond, brother of Blanche PARRY

Rowland VAUGHAN = Elizabeth PARRY
of Porthaml heiress, b. 1531
m.bef.1545

Watkyn VAUGHAN = Joan PARRY
of Bredwardine, b. 1530
m.bef.1545

Griffith JONES = (1) Jane PARRY (2) = (1) Robert (2) = Elizabeth
of Llowes, m.bef.1573 d.c.1597 VAUGHAN
d. 1577/8 d.c.1599

Elizabeth VAUGHAN = (1) **Rowland VAUGHAN** (2) = Anne JONES
b.aft.1561 b.c.1558/9, d.1627 m.c.1593-5
m.c.1582, d.c.1588 coheiress of
heiress of Newcourt Whitehouse

(3) = Elizabeth PROSSER
m. 1613, d. 1640
[later the wife of
Richard Leighton]

Epiphan HOWORTH = Blanche JONES
b.c.1567 coheiress of Whitehouse
d.bef.Apr 1649

John VAUGHAN
b.c.1583
student at The Inner
Temple 1605,
Gent. of Whitehouse,
1630

William VAUGHAN
named 1599 as exor.
to Robert VAUGHAN

others

Richard
VAUGHAN
d.bef. 1624

Elizabeth
VAUGHAN
of age by 1627
m. by 1630
[to ... Davenport]

Katherine
VAUGHAN
of age by 1627

William VAUGHAN
of Peterchurch;
named (with his mother) in
a grant of land in 1632

Pedigree chart showing Rowland's wives and children, plus the Jones-Howorth connection

up all five children, of whom John, as the eldest son of his first wife, received most of his father's attention. He enrolled the boy at the age of 14 at Jesus College, Oxford and in 1605 at the Inner Temple, at that time the most fashionable of the London Inns of Court.[27] Anne had brought him a recently built country mansion set among water-meadows, and on these he set about forming a larger irrigation scheme in 1604 about which, to arouse publicity, he began to write *His Booke.* It was, of course, all rather expensive but his marriage to Anne had also brought him a new source of funding within the family. In 1604 he borrowed £400 from Epiphan Howorth.

Rowland's ambitions and optimism were typical of that vigorous age. From his time in London he would have witnessed opportunities for advancement and learnt to discard failures and move on. He was now prepared, perhaps with a hint of arrogance, to focus on enlarging and improving his estate and obtaining a status and reputation. Two factors were essential: wealth and a patron.

6 DROWNING THE VALLEY: THE NORTHERN SECTION FROM PETERCHURCH TO TURNASTONE

In the management of water-meadow systems an old saying by 'drowners' points out that 'You lets the water in at a trot and out at a gallop',[1] which has the effect both of providing an even depth of flow, and of maintaining the oxygen status in the irrigating water. In Rowland's scheme, as described in Chapter 4, the ridging-up of the alluvium to create the bedworks was intended to provide such a steady and relatively rapid flow, and an even coverage, ideally to a depth of around 25mm above the root zone of the sward, leaving much of the aerial parts of the plants above the water level. The bedworks were typically made up of low (0.5-1m high) ridges which varied from 6 to 10m wide. A hybrid form was developed in the Dore valley, where the alluvial soils and underlying gravels not only provided a firm base for the construction of the 'panes' for distributing the water, but also greatly assisted drainage in the central area of Rowland's waterworks. These sandy soils are more effective than clay/loam soils in conducting water and provide the best matrix for water-meadow flooding.

Maintaining a head of water is also crucial to the successful operation of a bedworks system of water-meadows. At the point of irrigation, the water needs to be at least a metre above the level of the river, which requires the water to be carried along leats with a gradient less than the river valley itself. The main carriers therefore need to be relatively long and the gradient of the river needs to maintain a steady fall along its length. In the Dore valley the floodplain falls from 120m above sea level just south of Peterchurch to 90m at Bacton. This represents a fall of 30m over a length of 6 kilometres and a very gentle average gradient of 1:200, which is reflected in the way the Dore meanders over its flood plain and is liable to natural flooding. The Trench Royal was developed by Rowland to provide a more secure flow which could be used to control the drainage pattern of the Dore and provide managed flood waters when needed.

The relationship between the layout of the various water-meadow systems and the pattern of river channels also reflects the underlying pattern of water distribution and the varying widths of the floodplain. In the Dore valley between Peterchurch and Turnastone, the main carrier, the Trench Royal, acted both as a drain and a feeder in different parts of the system. Where the Trench Royal ran below the feeder trench linking the Trenant brook to the Shegear brook it acted as a drain for land to the west of the Trench Royal at Poston. Between Poston and Turnastone, where the Trench Royal ran west of the original river course, the Trench acted as a distributor channel for the hybrid bedwork on the flat alluvial plain between it and the river Dore. At Turnastone, it was originally joined by the Slough brook and its floodplain across the widest part of the system between Poston, Turnastone and Chanstone Court. The Slough brook

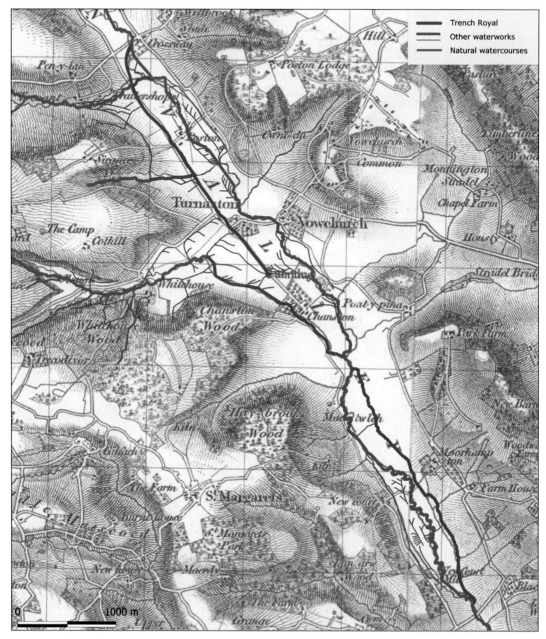

Map 6.1 Relief and natural drainage in the Golden Valley and the waterworks overlaid on first edition OS 1" to the mile,[2] 1830-1833.
(© Cassini Publishing Ltd, reproduced here by the kind permission of the publishers)

was subsequently diverted to the south across Weeth's meadow, possibly to reduce flooding in Turnastone village. A second diversion was later implemented, to its present course behind Chanstone Court, as described in Chapter 9.

The main features of the natural drainage and the artificial drainage and distribution channels developed by Rowland are shown in Map 6.1, where the narrow red lines show how water from the tributary brooks (shown blue) was captured and spread over the lowland area to the Trench Royal.

An overview of Rowland's waterworks in the Golden Valley

The GVSG project team undertook a series of field surveys in 2000 and 2012 with the aim of identifying what remained of Rowland's waterworks. The outputs of this survey have been compared with LIDAR[3] images to provide an integrated interpretation,[4] and the updated map of the overall system is shown in Chapter 9 (Map 9.1) which describes the remains in detail. This provides an update to the survey first completed by Penelope Wood in her undergraduate dissertation *Water Control in the Golden Valley, Herefordshire* of 1943.

Ascertaining which features are connected with the waterworks is not straightforward. Penelope Wood comments that Rowland's account in *His Booke* does not give any place-names and it is difficult to derive, with any certainty, a full description of the layout and how it operated. There is no original map of the scheme relating the different elements of the water management system with the land uses, topography, or the actual course of the Dore and its tributaries. However, a hand-drawn map in her dissertation makes a very useful attempt to place the different elements of the system in their geographical context (Map 6.2).

The map shows how the waterworks sit within the landscape in relationship to the natural drainage patterns in this part of the Dore valley. The upland features are defined by the shaded contours rising from 125m above sea level in the valley floor to 250-300m or more in the adjacent uplands. The course of the river Dore is shown winding across the valley floor and is distinguished from the water features associated with the hybrid bedworks irrigation system by their straighter lines, the 'finger patterns' associated with distributor and drainage channels for 'floating' the irrigation water over the meadows, and the retaining terraces used to spread the water as it was distributed across the sloping fields.

The major tributaries and springs are shown rising in the west, and the Trenant, Shegear and Slough brooks cut steeper sided valleys, which have also been integrated into the system using a catchwork system to irrigate the land on the west side of the Trench Royal away from the river. In this system water from the springs was channelled along the contours, overflowing to flood the sloping fields and draining back to the Trench Royal.

The main structural elements of the water management system consisted of: the main weir and sluices just south of Peterchurch, which diverted the river flows into the most significant feature in the system – the 'Trench Royal'; a second weir located in the Dore about 800m downstream of the main weir; a third weir located a further 1,500m downstream near Bacton, and two main categories of distributor trenches which served to spread the water over the meadows: bedworks and catchworks.

The Trench Royal formed a channel with a fall of 11m over a distance of 3 kilometres between Peterchurch and Turnanstone/Chanstone in a south-easterly direction (a gradient of 1:270). It broadly followed the 120m contour, approximately 200m to the west of the Dore.

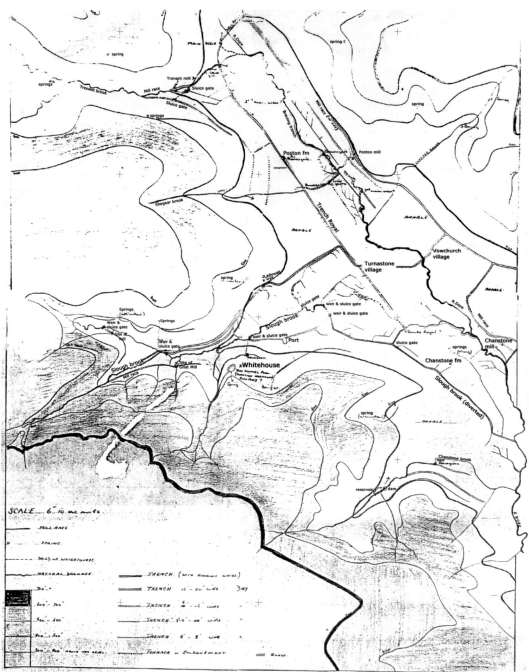

Map 6.2 *Rowland's waterworks in the Turnastone area (from Penelope Wood, 1943).*
The map shows the upland features of the valley with shaded contours (some shading is lost in reproduction) and the major streams flowing into the Dore. The man-made 'trenches' of differing sizes have straighter lines and finger patterns. The retaining terraces spread and distributed water across the sloping fields. Mill leats, weirs and sluices controlled the water flows.
Note, some terraces and water features have subsequently been eroded.

Water was raised into the upstream end of the Trench Royal and was regulated by floodgates immediately above the main weir to control the water levels in the Trench. The canal kept its altitude throughout its length so that the land between itself and the river could be flooded. For its first 800m the Trench Royal was 5m wide and almost 3m deep. The remainder of the canal then narrowed to 3m and just over 1m deep (Fig. 6.1).

This evidence closely follows the description given by Rowland in *His Booke*. This and the following quotations are not verbatim but have been paraphrased into a more accessible form of modern English: 'In building my Trench Royal, not only did I level it from start to finish at ground level, but also levelled the bottom of the trench to avoid error. The main part of the trench, 2½ miles long, is 10ft wide and 4ft deep, plus half a mile at the start at 8ft depth, and sometimes 16ft wide, in order to convey more water to the drowning grounds.'

The second weir, about 800m downstream from the first weir, 'commanded' water from the river Dore into the 'Braving Trench'. This smaller trench was almost 1m wide and 0.5m deep and ran for several kilometres following the course of the river at a distance of about 2m from the bank along the levee close to the river. This land, adjacent to the river, was raised by flood sedimentation from the river. The bank operated like the Trench Royal and the meadows could only be flooded from the river by managed flows from the Braving Trench through a system of irrigation channels. Earth excavated to form the Braving Trench was thrown up against the river bank as an additional protection against natural flooding. The flood water was eventually drained back into the river through a series of drainage channels. The evidence for this has largely been lost by subsequent erosion and deposition (see Chapter 9 for LIDAR evidence).

Rowland also comments on the dimensions of the braving trench or 'topping trench' and its construction: 'I should also mention the two-foot topping trench, parallel to and within 4 or 5 feet of the main river, and supplied from a weir or sluice in the river at its upper end. This trench provides a supply of water at the river bank (which is considerably higher than the river

Fig. 6.1 Trench Royal between Poston Court and Turnastone

bottom) for times when the river is low. In winter, this is drowned with the rest of the land, but in summer it can be used to provide controlled drowning for just half or a quarter of an hour. ... The braving (topping) trench should be used every morning in hot summers. In extreme heat you may need to resort to double drowning.'

The third weir, located a further 1500m down the main river near Bacton, was probably used to flood the opposite side of the valley. This part of the system was described in Chapter 4, and was not included in Penelope Wood's analysis of 1943.

Rowland comments in *His Booke* that there was no evidence on the ground that this type of water management had been done previously in this part of the Golden Valley. 'Being persuaded of the excellence of the water, I examined the foot fall from my mill to the uppermost part of my grounds, being a measured mile in length. There were 30 acres of old meadow ground, heavily laden with moss, cowslips and many other imperfect grasses, between my millstream and the main river. My grandfather could have drowned this land for just two shillings, but there was no evidence, from tradition or record, that this was ever done.'

The second part of the system around Whitehouse, Poston Court and the Turnastone lands would have been developed after 1593-95 when Rowland's second marriage to Anne Jones, heiress of the Whitehouse estate, enabled him to extend his waterworks in the Slough valley. He retained the right to live at Newcourt after his first wife's death in 1587 and only moved to Whitehouse in 1612. In 1607 he also secured the rights to a range of property from John Parry of Poston, whose estates in the Golden Valley extended over lands in Vowchurch and Turnastone and the sheep grazing uplands of Turnastone (see Chapter 7). The major feature of this development was the Trench Royal, which intercepted three main tributaries of the Dore – the Trenant, Shegear and Slough brooks – enabling additional volumes of water to be drawn into the main trench from these sources or directed by sluices into the main river. Weirs and sluices were also used to divert the streams on these rivers to serve a complex system of smaller trenches, from which the land to the west of the Trench Royal was flooded. The evidence for this is particularly striking in the terraced slopes opposite Poston Court (see Chapter 9). Further downstream, the brooks fed back into the river Dore and the Trench Royal.

Rowland Vaughan's system of water irrigation shows a keen understanding of the potential for the juxtaposition of fast-flowing upland streams feeding the more mature river Dore to provide opportunities for capturing the river flows and controlling their release over the flatter valley bottoms. It was also used to manage the flows to prevent flash flooding, which is a characteristic of these streams during periods of heavy rainfall in the autumn and spring. The system also takes advantage of the gentle slopes of the adjacent river terraces by using the slope to enhance the irrigation flows and drainage of the meadows in the valley bottom.

He comments in *His Booke* that whilst he was always looking to learn from others, there were no other schemes which had put into practice his principles of water management: 'Since I first undertook the drowning of my grounds I have always sought to improve my understanding through others' experience, and yet on this matter I found no workable observations to be had. Indeed I cannot understand why so many farmers allow rivers and other waterways to wash away into the sea so much goodness from their soils. Both arable and pasture lands could benefit hugely from drowning, as seen in the case of those areas that flood naturally. Given the ample supply of water in Wales, and the nature of its soils, I believe the principality could become the "garden of England".'[5]

This further illustrates that whilst Rowland may not have invented the concept of a sophisticated water management system, the publication of *His Booke* closely identifies him with its practical application and an elaboration of its principles and practices for the first time. It also illustrates his concern that no other farmers seemed to have adopted water management systems that conserve the land and its fertility. He was very much aware of the importance of the types of soils needed for good water management and the drowning regime for different seasons and he advised, 'Take account of your soil, for sandy ground will take ten times more water than will clay. Excessive water on clay soils, especially in summer, can cause lasting damage to the fertility. If there has been insufficient summer rain, then a moderate drowning with clear water may be beneficial, just 1-3 days before mowing. This will soften the roots and produce high quality hay. This controlled drowning is facilitated by the level trench royal, which enables you to channel the water to wherever it is needed.'

Penelope Wood also distinguished two main categories of distributor trenches which served to spread the water over the meadows. The first was a series of hybrid bedwork trenches which conveyed water to feed the whole of the valley floor (controlled by the weir on the Trench Royal) encompassing the land on the flood plain below the 120 metre contour. These trenches ran for about 250m according to the area of ground to be flooded, and decreased in size as they proceed from the 'commanding' trench, whilst others closely resembled the 'courier' trenches on the Trench Royal. The evidence for this kind of irrigation is found today in the valley floor between Peterchurch and Turnastone between the Trench Royal and the river Dore and is best preserved in the meadows around Poston Court and Turnastone Farm, where it has not been degraded by subsequent arable farming and associated ploughing (see Chapter 9).

She also identified the catchwork systems used on the slopes of the adjacent hills and valleys to irrigate the land on the far side of the Trench Royal from the river. They were most well developed in the upper slopes of the Slough brook, which also fed the bedworks on the level fields near Ladywell and around Turnastone in the valley below. In this system, the trenches conveying water to flood gently rising ground or hillsides, were drained either from the same stream, higher up the valley, or from the main trenches, or from the springs. They were intended more for summer drownings than for winter flooding, and were only small in scale – up to 2.5m wide at the most. Only small volumes of water were used on the lower slopes to prevent soil erosion.

The courses of many of the trenches were often dug alongside existing natural boundaries and these may now be marked by hedges established since the trenches fell out of use. The hedges may also have drainage ditches thrown out beside a hedge, but Penelope Wood suggested that one may distinguish the irrigation trenches from ditches because the trenches had controlled gradients to obtain a gradual fall. There were no banks on either side of the trenches compared to the retaining banks on the ditches because the surplus soil was used to fill in hollows in the fields to smooth out field gradients. The trenches were constructed to a definite width and depth and were not often straight but curved to follow the contours.

The most well developed bedwork systems are associated with the chalk-rivers of southern England, whose valleys generally contain extensive spreads of post-glacial gravels. The importance of the storage capacity of the chalk aquifers is to provide a reliable flow in the main waterways. This dampens the peak-flows and sustains base-flow in rivers when compared to areas of impermeable catchments, where flooding presents greater problems, as noted by Ward

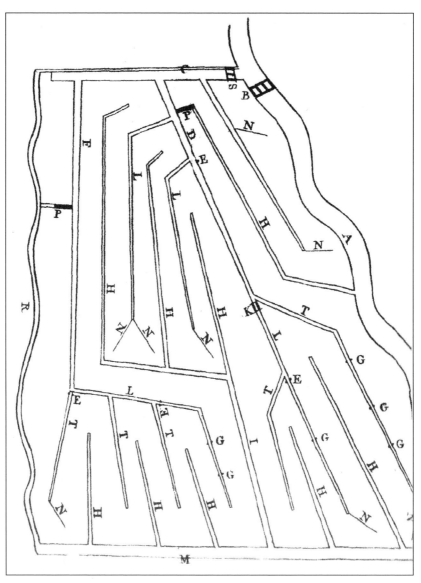

Fig. 6.2 Schematic bedwork system (from Boswell, 1779).
In Boswell's system the meadow was watered by a stream running on one side (A), while a weir (B) and sluice (S) directed water into the head main (C), with smaller mains (D) and (F) taken out of the head main. Bends (E) in the smaller mains and branch trenches (T) checked the water and ensured its distribution throughout the system. Further bends (G) slowed down the rate of flow and spread it across the meadow. Trench drains (H) on each side of every distribution channel (T) drained the water from the panes. Sluice drains (P) carried leakages out of the main trenches D and F. The secondary distribution channels L, T and N spread the water over the meadow and the smallest gutters (N) carried water to the longest corners of the panes. The drainage was controlled via a 'master' drain (I) which collected the water from several drainage channels and discharged into the 'tail drain' (M) which then discharged into the river.

and Robinson.[6] The silt deposition of chalk streams also provided an ideal way of adding nutrients to the soil without the problem of acidification, because of the buffering effect of dissolved calcium maintaining a balance to the acidity of the soils. However, the system developed in the Dore valley, where adjacent limestone springs provided calcareous water and a buffer to smooth out peak and low flows, also had the advantage of alluvial soils and underlying gravels to provide a firm base for the construction of the 'panes' for distributing the water. This system assisted drainage in the central area of Rowland's waterworks and enabled an early form of hybrid bedworks to be developed.

Together with the associated irrigation and drainage channels, the waters diverted by the sluices and weirs formed an integrated system which Rowland estimates in *His Booke* could be used to flood about 300 acres: 'I had my servant, a joiner, to make a level to discover how much land I could cover from the entry point of the water, which turned out to be some 300 acres.' However, the innovations met with considerable opposition from tenants, neighbours and friends in the Golden Valley and he comments: 'Having begun the work, the inhabitants of the Golden Valley summoned a consultation against me and my man, John the leveller, saying our wits were in our hands not our heads. We suffered 3-4 years of mockery for our engineering methods that their forefathers had not experienced'. The relationship between Rowland and his joiner deteriorated over time, and when he found that the joiner was taking credit for his innovation, he sacked him. Rowland comments: 'People began to show interest and commendation as the work progressed, and the joiner/leveller became boastful, claiming to be a party to the invention which in truth was all mine.'[7] Rowland was jealously guarding his reputation as 'the man who drowned the meadows'.

Did Vaughan's work influence schemes elsewhere?

In his treatise of 1779,[8] George Boswell developed a comprehensive account of the most sophisticated developments of water-meadow irrigation as they had developed in the chalklands of southern England in the 18th century. He describes the principles of water management: how land is properly adapted for watering and the methods for laying out the irrigation/drainage systems in different natural conditions. The illustration from his book (Fig. 6.2) shows a particular set of drainage channels which, to some extent, reflect the pattern developed earlier by Rowland in the Golden Valley.

A feature of Boswell's system, which he shared with Rowland's approach, was the equal emphasis given to both the irrigation and drainage functions for the efficient flows of water across the system. They both emphasised the need for irrigation channels to have bends in the smaller 'mains' and ' branch' trenches to slow down the rate of flow and spread water across the meadow. These checks in the rate of flow ensured its distribution throughout the system, aided by the use of secondary distribution channels in a hierarchy of different sized channels and the small 'gutters' which extended to the extremities of the meadow. In both systems, the drainage was controlled via a 'master' drain which collected the water from several drainage channels and discharged into the 'tail drain' which then discharged into the river.

In Rowland's 'water-workes' large areas of water flooding level ground were held back by low ridges. Between the ridges the land was carefully levelled, using spoil from the trench excavations to fill hollows in the ground. This formed a hybrid form of bedworks which was more like a 'floating upwards' system of water-meadow irrigation than the more fully developed bedwork systems of water distribution and drainage channels found in the floodplains of the chalkland rivers of Dorset and Wiltshire in the 17th and 18th centuries.

7   ROWLAND VAUGHAN, THE CHURCH AND FAMILY LIFE

When Rowland was born people of his parents' age would have had clear memories of Henry VIII withdrawing the Church in England from the rule of the Pope only 25 years earlier. In the Golden Valley they would have witnessed the dissolution of Dore Abbey three years later, followed by the Crown's handover of its estates and goods to the local gentry such as Baskerville, Parry, Scudamore and Vaughan. They had lived through the religious swings of Protestant reformists followed by the Catholicism of Queen Mary and her husband, King Philip II of Spain, to reach the uneasy Protestant settlement of Elizabeth I when she came to the throne in 1558, the year of Rowland's birth. Faced as Elizabeth was with internal plots and foreign threats, her subjects might well have expected her reign to last no more than a few years, leaving the nation without a direct heir and open to the return of a Catholic monarch. Throughout Rowland's lifetime religious beliefs were always present in both daily affairs and politics, with the church wielding power over both ecclesiastical and moral matters through its own courts. His home lay in a countryside where there were many Catholic families as well as some extreme reformists. He himself was brought up as a staunch Protestant openly supporting the Crown, declaring in 1610 to Lord Pembroke, 'Your Lordship doth see I am no Papist, nor Puritane, but a true Protestant according to the Kings Injunctions.'[1]

By the end of Elizabeth I's reign in 1603 the government was faced not only with extremist Catholic insurgents but also the growing strength of the Puritans, especially those in Parliament. The penal legislation against recusant Catholics introduced earlier in the queen's reign was quietly eased, with the pope demanding 'quietness' and James I preferring 'accommodation over persecution'.[2] Catholics and their seminary priests loyal to the Crown were less systematically harassed, unlike the militant Jesuit missionaries travelling the country trying to stir up revolt. Even church leaders held differing views, with the archbishop of Canterbury, Richard Bancroft, aiming to bring loyalist Catholics into the Church of England whilst Bishop Robert Bennett of Hereford was a strict reformist. Among the laity some Herefordshire magistrates were unwilling to take action against their Catholic neighbours, so that Catholic gentry loyal to the Crown, like Baskerville of Eardisley, Seabourne of Stretton Sugwas, and John Parry and Richard Davies living at or near Poston, were left quietly to continue their Catholic worship.[3]

Rowland, however, had little sympathy for the extremists and in 1603 he was involved with his elder brother Henry, also a Herefordshire magistrate as well as Lieutenant of Breconshire, in capturing the plotter William Watson, organiser of the Bye Plot, a madcap Catholic attack planned on London mounted from the Welsh Marches. In his band were John Parry of Poston and an unnamed Vaughan. The attempt fizzled out and Watson fled to hide in south Wales only to be recognised and caught outside Hay (or, according to another report, near Abergavenny) by the Vaughan brothers, Henry and Rowland. Watson was subsequently executed.[4]

Two years later, in May 1605, a riot occurred nearer home at Allensmore when the vicar refused a place of burial for a Catholic parishioner. A crowd led by the local seminary priest Roger Cadwallader arrived soon after daybreak on the Tuesday after Whitsun to dig the grave and perform the burial.[5] The vicar, aroused from his bed, was too late to stop it. The dispute flared across the district among the Catholics centred nearby at Whitfield and Treville and, more especially, those on the Monmouthshire border a few miles away around the larger Catholic community centred upon The Cwm at Llanrothal. It was not until 19 June that order was fully restored after four Herefordshire magistrates, supporting Bishop Bennett and including Rowland, took a strong force to search Llanrothal village and the adjacent dense woodland (Fig. 7.1) throughout that night and the following day. They found much evidence of Catholic worship, but the inhabitants had all fled across the nearby river Monnow into the safety of Wales and beyond the reach of the Herefordshire officials.[6] Within a few months the disorder in west Herefordshire was forgotten in the wider uproar caused by the Gunpowder Plot to blow up king and Parliament.

It is strange that in *His Booke* addressed to Lord Pembroke Rowland does not refer to his part in the Llanrothal event, but the upheavals had little lasting effect and by 1610 the Catholic threat was diminishing. The villagers had returned to Llanrothal, and life in Herefordshire was restored to its previous pattern. Archdeacons carried out their routine visitations of the

Fig. 7.1 The Cwm, Llanrothal

parishes, receiving the reports of clergy and churchwardens of the frequent cases of adultery, sexual intercourse outside wedlock, churches in poor repair and lacking the required books, registers and homilies, unlicensed parsons, the occasional farmer at work on the Sabbath, and parishioners failing to attend church services.[7] Among these last were named Catholic recusants whom Rowland dismissed as 'a few of the simpler sort, more inclined to Masse then to sound Religion'.[8] In the period from 1611 they included Richard Parry, gentleman, Mary wife of Thomas Vaughan, both of Peterchurch, who must have been well known to Rowland, and in 1625 Thomas and Katherine Prosser of Vowchurch, who probably were his own wife's uncle and aunt.

As he extended his property, Rowland held the advowsons (the right as patron to nominate the parish priest) not only of Bacton (until about 1611) but also of Turnastone, Vowchurch and Peterchurch, receiving their annual tithes of crops and livestock and becoming responsible for the repair of the church chancels and the nomination of parochial clergy for installation by the Bishop of Hereford. These matters caused him endless trouble. Nevertheless, he held to his beliefs in choosing parish clergy, looking for conforming Protestant preachers, not always with success. At Peterchurch there was 'an old Monke upon the dissolution of the Abbey of Doier, that was cast from thence ... so spoyling the Scripture with idle intentions, that at his end he left neither Protestant, Puritane Nor Papist'.[9] This was William Marbury (variously spelt), one of the abbey's ten monks at the dissolution. He had been appointed by George Parry in 1563, remaining at Peterchurch until his death in about 1595 when he was still not licensed, not catechising the members of his congregation and not keeping the vicarage in repair.

Rowland replaced him as vicar of Peterchurch with Thomas Barnsley, an Oxford-educated and newly ordained priest, with a reputation as a preacher, and by 1598 had appointed him as curate of Bacton. It proved to be a poor choice. Rowland devoted several pages in *His Booke*[10] to complain about Barnsley's unsuitability as a parish priest, paucity of sermons as a preacher and indulgence in exorbitant money-lending and by 1608 succeeded in removing him. Barnsley, however, remained firmly in the Golden Valley, being presented by John Parry in 1604 to the rectory of Turnastone, which he held with the curacy of Vowchurch from at least 1615. There must still have been some close accord between him and Rowland, for one of the latter's last acts in May 1626, shortly before his death, was to grant Barnsley the advowson of Turnastone for services rendered in many dealings. The situation was similar in neighbouring parishes. The new vicar of Peterchurch from 1608 to at least 1630 likewise never preached a single sermon nor catechised his parishioners, whilst Thomas Baskerville, serving as vicar of Vowchurch and curate of Turnastone from 1586 until 1612-13, was reported by the churchwardens for not being licensed, not preaching and his churches lacking the required books.[11] At Vowchurch a Richard Vaughan was recorded in 1615 as a short-term vicar. He may have been Rowland's younger son but his ordination and licence have not been found and he does not appear again.[12]

With such a genuine shortage of adequately paid and trained clergy it is unsurprising that Rowland claimed that in the area there were 'foure and twenty parishes; not any one of all able to maintain a Preaching Minister [so that] There were not two Sermons in the Golden-Vale this 500 yeares'.[13] With Peterchurch, Vowchurch and Turnastone in the gift respectively of the bishop, the dean and chapter of Hereford and himself, he thought it would be a good opportunity to put forward an Act of Parliament to unite them. Bishop Bennett appeared supportive but neither he nor Lord Pembroke took any action. Nor was his suggestion favoured locally.

The Puritans saw it as restricting their aims, the congregations grumbled that the churches were not large enough to hold all of them together – pointing out that although all three churches were within a mile or so of each other their outlying parishioners lived miles apart, and everyone took it as just another example of Rowland's 'ambition; seeking mine own glory and gaine'.[14]

Throughout the years that Rowland was responsible for the upkeep of the churches he was repeatedly charged to carry out repairs. For example, in 1609, when the vicar of Peterchurch, John Hopkins, was ordered to repair the damaged vicarage, Rowland was required to repair the church-yard wall and the ruinous chancel, then in a state of collapse, and the churchwardens were in trouble for not tolling the church bell 'because it was not their custom'. Two years

Fig. 7.2 The church and churchyard at Peterchurch are well kept and maintained in the 21st century, unlike in Rowland's time.

later the chancel had still not been repaired and the churchyard remained unfenced with the result 'that swine come in and dig the graves most grievously to behold'.[15] He admitted in *His Booke* that the church (presumably Peterchurch) 'is downe' but by then he could not afford to rebuild the chancel. The demands for repair were still being repeated to John Hopkins in 1614. At Vowchurch, where in 1605 the chancel was also described as very ruinous and the church lacked a Bible, Book of Common Prayer or other service book, a remarkable if crude timber screen between nave and chancel was erected and dated 1613.[16] The same year is inscribed on Rowland's coat of arms displayed in the nave at Vowchurch (see Fig. 8.2 in Chapter 8), which implies his involvement in the Jacobean timberwork there.

In addition to these public difficulties and the enlargement of his *water-workes*, Rowland's relatively brief marriage with Anne Jones (*c.*1593/95 to *c.*1606) also coincided with the matri-monial problems of his niece Joan Winstone, whom he called his 'Welch neece' (a colloquial description for a family member living out of social contact or far away), which erupted in a lawsuit in 1605 and which with good reason he blamed for the financial problems that haunted the rest of his life.[17]

The story begins with the marriage in 1579 of Rowland's elder sister Elizabeth to Sir Henry Winston of Standish in Gloucestershire. By 1586 they had five children, of whom four survived childhood – Henry, William, Joan (1584-1630) and Jane.[18] After their mother's early death the children were sent to live with their Vaughan relatives at Bredwardine. Sir Henry married secondly, about 1589, Diones or Denise (variously spelt), daughter of Sir George Bond of London, who bore him a further eight children. The Vaughan children now returned to Standish to be brought up with their half siblings in what proved to be an uneasy household. Their stepmother is said to have hated everything to do with the Vaughans, treating the children cruelly, particularly when their father was away from home, by locking them up in a cold room, giving them only one candle at mealtime and keeping them so short of clothes that young Jane had to go about bare-legged. The accusation is borne out by the fact that years later the eldest son and heir, Henry, left instructions in his will to be buried not at Standish but at his mother's family homeland of Bredwardine.[19] Finally the two girls tried to run away, news of their plight reached Herefordshire, and Uncle Rowland rode to the rescue and took them back to live at Bredwardine again.

Sir Henry was not pleased with this arrangement and refused to contribute anything towards the girls' upkeep, claiming that the Vaughans had deliberately made them unmanageable and taught them to 'play the runagates'. However he had previously been sufficiently concerned for his first wife's children to provide a copyhold property on the estate for William and his sisters, Joan and Jane, as a source of income, to be held by them for their lifetimes successively. It was this arrangement which exacerbated the trouble in the unhappy family. In the first place the two girls were still living with their grandmother in Herefordshire. Secondly, William married and shortly afterwards died, leaving his widow in possession of the copyhold estate. This provoked Joan to return to Standish to claim the property for herself as the next 'life' under the terms of the grant and to put in a Herefordshire tenant, Christopher Berrows, which led to her father forcing an eviction and, as a magistrate, putting her and her supporters into Gloucester gaol for breaking the law. Other friends bailed her out and her uncle Rowland seized the opportunity to reinforce his role as her guardian and take Sir Henry Winston to court in 1605-6.[20]

Rowland was probably attracted by the chance of managing her affairs and she remained in his household for three years, during which time he took her up to London. There she again exhibited her independence, for she met and married John Walcot[21]

Fig. 7.3 The Court of Wards and Liveries in Session. (By permission of and © the Trustees of the Goodwood Collection)

without seeking either her father's or Rowland's permission. Winston was angry and Rowland was accused of failing in his duties as guardian, although by then she must have been over the age of 21. Nevertheless, he was harried in a series of lawsuits in Chancery, Star Chamber and the Court of Wards and Liveries in the course of which Sir Henry died in 1609. The case rumbled on for five years in which, as Rowland put it, the Court of Wards 'bredd more white haires in my head in one yeare, then all my Wetshod-water-workes did in sixteene'.[22]

The story also destroys the concept of Rowland as the country landowner, settled with wife and family in rural Herefordshire and taking part only in county affairs and the improvement of his estates. Not only had he spent a few years as a young man at Queen Elizabeth's court, but he was also familiar as a man about town, eventually involved in a string of at least 17 lawsuits heard in London. As he told Lord Pembroke, he could always be found at Master Wotton the

Map 7.1 Detail from John Norden's map of London, 1593. St Dunstan's in the West, opposite Rowland's lodgings in Fleet Street, is marked by the number 15, circled in red. (© The British Library Board, Maps.Crace.Port.1.33)

scrivener's in Fleet Street opposite St Dunstan's in the West church, or having supper at John Gents.[23] He was sufficiently well known around the law courts for the Lord Chief Justice Sir John Popham to draw him aside and ask about his waterworks, to which he must have replied at some length for the Lord Chief Justice then to comment in friendly disbelief 'Cousin, art thou out of thy witts'.[24]

The cost of Joan's affairs was heavy. Not only did Rowland run up life-long debts to London money lenders, which resulted in his only narrowly avoiding arrest for imprisonment on a legal technicality but also, as he explained to Lord Herbert, he was obliged to neglect the construction of the waterworks with the result that his head carpenter had carried out the work so badly that much of it had to be redone.[25] On the one occasion when he returned home to Herefordshire, he left Joan in the care of a 'sanctimonious Puritan tailor' he thought he could trust to keep her out of mischief – only to learn that in his absence 'hee married my Welch Neece to his English Nephew'.[26]

Rowland reacted surprisingly calmly to the tailor's protest that the marriage had occurred without his knowledge. Maybe in *His Booke* he deliberately avoided the name of the 'tailor' to conceal the fact that really he was aware that Joan's young husband was John Walcot, the nephew of a rich London merchant. Perhaps having spent at least £60 on the lawsuits Rowland was relieved to see Joan had made a good choice for herself. John Walcot lived in Fenchurch Street, close to the legal quarter of the city where he had entered Lincoln's Inn in the winter of 1602.[27] He came from a landowning family in Shropshire, his father had twice been sheriff of Brecon and his brother had married the daughter of Sir John Games, himself a relative of the Vaughans by marriage.[28] His uncle Humfrey (1545-1616) settled in London and became a wealthy merchant of the Company of Grocers. Rowland was reassured by the familiar names from the Welsh Marcher connections and the satisfying result avoided the wrath of the Court of Wards.[29] Some 20 years later he recalled how he expressed his approval 'For the betterment of their marriage' by selling three horses and delaying payment to his tailor, giving Walcot £90 with a bed and furniture worth £20, and presenting Joan with a £1 mirror and a fashionable lady's waist-coat for £20.[30]

The young couple flourished. Rowland, though, was ruined, and Walcot took an increasing part in his downfall. With his debts already mounting, Rowland never recovered from the effects of the legal expenses, his own costs of living in London and the bills of the London money lenders that had built up and spawned more litigation. This is reflected in changes at home. His son John did not take a degree at Jesus College as was permitted by the university, nor complete law studies at the Inner Temple which might cover a wide range of learned subjects.[31] In 1607 Rowland and his son John, both described as 'of Whitehouse', signed away their half-share of a house and lands in Peterchurch to Thomas Prosser, a farmer at Mowbach in Peterchurch, an action which suggests that Anne had died shortly before.[32] Rowland continued to occupy Newcourt until 1611-12, although by then he had extended his waterworks into the nearby Poston meadows and as Anne's widower had the use of Whitehouse. However he was not regularly called 'of Whitehouse' before 1614 and the move had evidently occurred at some time between 1611 and 1613.

By then Rowland had married his third wife, Elizabeth, daughter of Watkin Prosser, a Peterchurch tailor and ale-house keeper.[33] The wedding took place between 1611 and 27

November 1613, the date they were both summoned to appear before the church's consistory court for entering into a clandestine marriage. The nature of this misdemeanour is not explained. It might have been because the Prosser family included known Catholics, a failure to call the banns, or not marrying in the church. Or it might have been that their son William was born out of wedlock, probably in 1611. Neither of them attended the court on that occasion nor in the following year when the case was renewed, and they were excommunicated. Fortunately, Rowland was still in a position to seek favours for his earlier support of the bishop of Hereford and they obtained dispensation.[34]

The Prosser family, like the Parrys and Vaughans, were of Welsh origin and like them, their name was common in the neighbourhood where they had lived throughout the 16th century. As noted above, Rowland had in 1607 done business with Thomas Prosser over a farm at Mowbach in Peterchurch and in 1608 he was called in as a magistrate by Watkin Prosser of Peterchurch to settle a series of fights between Richard Parry and his family and the Prossers. The root of the trouble appears to have lain in the rowdiness and licensing of Parry's alehouse, which ended with the beating-up of Watkin Prosser and his wife Katherine and William Legge, one of Rowland's servants. On that occasion Rowland avoided getting involved beyond exchanging words with the Parrys during which Richard Parry claimed 'that it is well known that if the said Rowland Vaughan had not been advanced by marriages to great lands this defendant Richard Parry was by birth the same of a gentleman of equal qualitie with the father of Rowland Vaughan' and that he too had served in the wars. Parry's bitter ill-will concluded with the retort that Rowland 'was not then a magistrate', and therefore it was none

Fig. 7.4 Wilmaston farmhouse in Peterchurch

Fig. 7.5 Looking across the Golden Valley from above Wilmaston

of his business.[35] If true, this would explain Rowland's later rough-handling by some of the local men (see Chapter 8). As for Watkin Prosser and his wife, they claimed later in 1617 that they were Rowland's long-established household servants.

By now Rowland's disrespect for the law had been exhibited in litigation and unpaid debts, by failing to appear when summoned, ignoring demands for repayment, and in his third marriage openly ignoring the law. He was not unique. Elizabethan and Jacobean men of all classes were quick to start fights, draw their swords or take the law in their own hands. Within days of receiving the summons to attend the consistory court in Hereford he was visited at the Whitehouse before dawn by the county sheriff with a writ for his arrest for failing to pay a debt to Francis Pember, one of the local men to whom he was indebted. Vaughan did not go quietly. The sheriff and his men were assaulted by Rowland and his wife, Watkin Prosser of Vowchurch and his wife, with at least two other members of the Prosser family living close at hand and disturbed by the racket, together with others, some of whom, the sheriff claimed, were armed. Indeed, Watkin Prosser did admit that he had picked up a hedging billhook that he happened to have at hand. The sheriff and his men fled, leaving Rowland to chase them off in triumph at having defeated them. Subsequently, there were apologies and excuses of misunderstandings, with Rowland denying the sheriff's version of events and stating that he and Pember had already come to terms over the debt; there had been, he claimed, no reason for a writ against him and nothing riotous had occurred.[36]

Such was the start of Rowland and Elizabeth's married life. In their 18 years or so together Elizabeth had many problems to face, but the wording on her rather crude memorial stone in the church at Peterchurch (given at the end of Chapter 8), suggests a certain proud memory of their life. For Rowland, his new wife had the great attraction of being young, prepared to care for him, look after his existing family and able to bear him at least one more child, William.[37]

In 1614 Vaughan lived with his new family at Wilmaston, another manor house in Peterchurch parish, but from 1615 he is always described as 'of Whitehouse' and for the last years of his life he was engaged in legal battles and rough raids to hold on to it (see Chapter 8).[38]

8   'A very Polliticke Gent'

In her edition of *His Booke* in 1897 Ellen Beatrice Wood concluded her introduction with an imaginative description of Rowland in his old age: 'We must, then, fancy the old squire in his scarlet cape, riding-rod in hand, walking down the Golden Valley from the White House to New Court (some three miles) to overlook the raising of the sluices and the marshalling of his 'Mechanicalls' to dinner, ... reading the Riot Act to the unruly, and intermeddling with kindly officiousness in the private matters of his people'.[1]

Not so, for archival evidence shatters this glowing picture. The whole tragic story of the last years of his life is exposed in two supplications that Rowland laid before the court of Chancery in 1623 and 1625.[2] Both documents fill several huge closely written sheets of parchment, torn and stained with the dirt of four centuries. In these he put his complaints in the same rambling and repetitive style as *His Booke*. The story that unfolds is one of complex debts and mortgages, heard not only in Chancery, where Rowland himself stretched out the hearings by sometimes failing to attend, but also in the related cases which he brought before Star Chamber (where personal attendance was replaced by information in writing) and to the President of the Council of the Marches in Wales, where they remained unresolved.

Rowland, it must be remembered, was not wealthy. From the very beginning of his first marriage he was engaged in expensive litigation. He subsequently embarked on drowning his water-meadows, an undertaking that contemporary landowners acknowledged was a costly task, establishing one of the new style of forges inconveniently far from the sources of iron ore needed to feed it, and buying property that he claimed was worth up to £1,200 a year. All of this had only been achieved by heavy borrowing. Among his traceable debts were those he still owed to London money lenders as well as the mounting number of his family and Herefordshire neighbours. They varied or were passed from one to another so frequently that it becomes impossible to calculate their total sum. His three closest relatives became personally involved – his elder brother Henry Vaughan, his brother-in-law Epiphan Howorth, and John Walcot, the husband of his 'Welsh niece'. In the period between 1603 and 1612 they seem to have genuinely tried to save him, but when he failed to change his ways they became more concerned to protect their own interests and seize pickings for themselves. From 1614-15 their terms became more demanding. By the time of his death in 1627 he had lost the wide spread of his landed property and had nothing to leave his surviving son and two daughters.

Money became so central to his growing problems that it may be helpful to put some specific prices in 1600 in comparison with those of today. In 1607 a bricklayer or labourer in Essex earned 6d a day (2.5p) plus meat and drink. Away from London the rate was only 4d a day, the figure agreed by Rowland's own carpenter for the waterworks. Assuming that he was fully employed he might therefore have earned 24d (equivalent to about £10 in 2005) for six days work. However, it is actually extremely difficult to compare living costs over time. For instance, a Dartmouth master carpenter received 7d a day, plus a daily allotment of meat and drink, and worked a six-day week.[3] Today, an experienced bricklayer might expect about 1,100 times as much in pay, probably in a shorter working week.[4] In addition, while the value of the £ has decreased, the value of commodities such as land has changed due to supply and demand. So Rowland paid John Parry £310 in 1607 (equivalent to £31,000 in 2005) for the Poston estate stretching from Whitewall above Dolward farm to 'Poston Hill', together with the advowson of Turnastone.[5] In 2001 Turnastone Court Farm alone, consisting of just the low-lying central part of Parry's Poston estate, was sold at auction for £1¼ million.

As early as 1603-04 his brother Henry had attempted to organise Rowland's debts by raising a loan of £2,000, composed of £1,200 from himself, £400 from Epiphan Howorth, £300 from Walter Lloyd and £100 from Kinnard Delabere of Urishay.[6] Rowland pledged to pay his brother £400 a year at an exorbitant rate of 10% and more, using Newcourt as security for the payment. Over the next six or seven years Rowland did indeed pay back up to £1,700 but with the full settlement incomplete Henry Vaughan demanded £1,600 ready money and added £800 for a four-year extension of the loan. As a result Rowland calculated that the original loan would then have cost him a total of £3,620. Henry also refused to pass on to Howorth and Lloyd any payments which resided on the mortgage of Newcourt. Rowland had some grounds for complaining that his elder brother was acting 'maliciously and unconscionably'. In order to meet this fresh demand Rowland was driven in 1609 to take out a further 10-year mortgage from a new source. It would seem that Henry Vaughan was behind the arrangement by which James Husbands of Wormbridge provided this support whilst additional debts of over £1,887 owed to other lenders were secured by related mortgages obtained from William Pennyman and Edward Husbands. Between them they came to hold mortgages on all Rowland Vaughan's property, his interest in Newcourt, the former lands of John Parry of Poston in Vowchurch, Turnastone and St Margaret's and the Wilmaston estate in Peterchurch. Subsequently, in about 1610-11, Henry Vaughan and James Husbands gained possession of Wilmaston through the marriage settlement of Henry Vaughan's son and James Husband's daughter.[7]

All this was occurring at the peak of his life while he was still living at Newcourt with his second wife Anne. The strain of his financial affairs could not now be hidden and may, apart from his absence and expenses dealing with the marriage of his niece Joan, go to explaining the gap between the dates of the first draft of *His Booke* about 1604 and its revision and publication in 1610. For instance, he did not pay off the loan of £400 from Epiphan Howorth nor the second half of the £600 price for Herbert's Craswall Dairies and from 1599 he failed to a settle a £100 debt to William Vaughan, whose wages he had not paid for seven or eight years.[8] In 1607 he and his son John disposed of their interest in property at Mowbach in Peterchurch to the longstanding tenant Thomas Prosser,[9] and the following year they assigned his mortgage on the Peterchurch rectory and tithes to Thomas Morgan of Blackmoor in Abbeydore, to whom in 1609 he mortgaged Hanley Court in Kingstone.[10] In the same year they sold the manor of Wormbridge, which he had acquired at some date after 1586, to Martin Leather and James Husbands, ancestors of the Clive family, present owners of the Whitfield estate.

By 1609 his debts to the London moneylenders had risen to £365. His niece's husband, John Walcot, reappeared on the scene to repay these debts within three years on the security of a 20-years lease of Whitehouse.[11] Walcot appointed Thomas Davies of the Inner Temple, possibly a relative of the Vaughans, and John Breinton of Stretton Sugwas near Hereford as fellow-trustees to receive the estimated £200 rents of the estate, pay off the debt and pass on the remainder for Rowland, his wife and children. Rowland, however, failed to ensure that if he did not receive his share of the rents he could recover possession of the property. Walcot also undertook to pay off a debt of £500 to Richard Meyricke of London, who was himself in prison for debt, a fate that was always hanging over Rowland.

Matters worsened. In the last years of Rowland being known as 'of Newcourt' in 1610-11, Henry Vaughan and James Husbands of Wormbridge got together to sell the manor of Bacton with Newcourt and its park to James Husbands, who was still holding it 12 years later. This cleared the Vaughan brothers' debts to Husbands but at the price of losing the meadows where Rowland had begun his *water-workes*. The sale marks the end of Rowland's original waterworks at Newcourt. There is no later written evidence for continuation of the Newcourt waterworks and the faint signs of trenches in a small part of the original area of the waterworks are noticeably less prominent than those upstream between Peterchurch and Turnastone (see Chapters 3 and 8).

The layers of debts, loans and mortgages become difficult to follow, not least because much of the information comes from Rowland's evidence given ten years later in the long Chancery lawsuits of the 1620s and relating to events 20 years earlier. Summarising briefly, in about 1613 for the sum of £374 he extended the earlier mortgage of Whitehouse to Walcot, Breinton and Davies for a further 20 years. At some time, about 1610-12, Henry Vaughan, Howorth and a partner named only as Lake obtained Wilmaston and conveyed it to James Carwardine to secure some of their and Rowland's tangled debts. In 1614 Rowland was also still ensnared with debts dating back to at least 1592 owed to Sir John Games. Despite all these losses early in 1615, he still retained an interest in his properties in Clodock, Howton and the Golden Valley, including Wilmaston, worth £100 a year in rents, which he now put in the hands of trustees, thereby losing control of it all.[12] More significantly, in February 1615 he released to John Parry, the former Clerk Comptroller of the Royal Household, 87 acres of meadows and other lands in Peterchurch. This second withdrawal would appear to mark a further abandonment of Rowland's *water-workes*. After John Parry died later that year, his cousin and heir, John Parry of Poston, sold the land in 1617, leaving Rowland holding perilously on to his remaining works on the Whitehouse estate, for which like Newcourt there is no later written evidence.

By 1615 John Walcot was managing Rowland's debts to the London moneylenders by setting up a trust composed of himself, Davies and Breinton, secured on the annual income of £100 from Rowland's lifetime holding of Whitehouse and other properties. It would seem that Walcot, with his sharper London experience, out-manoeuvred Rowland, who by 1625 was complaining that the trustees had over the years received rents up to a value of £3,000 in settlement of what had started as a £365 debt. Worse, because Rowland could still not meet the debts dependent upon the income from Whitehouse, the house itself was claimed by Epiphan Howorth, with the support of Walcot.[13] Rowland's mounting debts, evasions and lawsuits were, of course, well known locally and led to a loss of respect illustrated in events far removed from the orderly London law courts and the money-lending Herefordshire gentry. Swindled local men took the law into their own hands.

Rowland himself had boasted in 1613 that he and his servants had chased the sheriff's men out of Whitehouse. In other cases he was the victim. In 1615, at the time when Walcot was taking care of Rowland's London debts and the Parrys were recovering from him some of their property in the Golden Valley, the relatively minor matter of the wages so long owed to his servant William Vaughan prompted an outrage that is hard to imagine today. On the Tuesday after Easter William and his brothers-in-law, James and Christopher Berrowe of Jury Farm in Abbeydore, together with other local men including Thomas Baskerville, ambushed Rowland on his way along the road between Whitehouse and Peterchurch. With 40 accomplices armed with swords, pistol, staves and bills, they assaulted and threatened to shoot him before marching him off the five miles to Jury Farm, hatless – a particular insult as everyone wore a hat as a mark of rank or occupation. They then demanded that Rowland let them off debts of £200 they owed him and that he pay William the £100 he was owed. Rowland sent for his brother, who negotiated a compromise: the Berrowe brothers, as an act of goodwill, offered to transfer their £200 bond to Rowland's two daughters Elizabeth and Katherine, whilst Rowland would pay William £110 and give him a nag and 20 nobles (£13.33) in cash.

However, the conditions of the agreement were not met. On 17 June the same band came at daybreak to Wilmaston, where Rowland was then living, roused him out of bed and, having already applied to the county sheriff for a warrant to apprehend him for debt, marched him off, unarmed and without shoes, hat or cloak, through the woods and back pathways once again to Jury Farm. They claimed later in court that they had treated him gently, and one, William Turner of Abbeydore, said that he was in fact wearing doublet, hose, slippers and nightcap. Nevertheless, their action was deeply humiliating and doubtless a topic of local gossip.[14] Two years later a party of two dozen men, including Breinton and Howorth, were accused by Rowland of stealing corn and grain and breaking into Whitehouse. The poor condition of the parchment document renders it largely illegible, but one of the defendants, Thomas Philpotts, vigorously denied the accusation with his clear retort 'that the said Complainant by trublesome suytes and other unthrifty Courses hath wasted and Consumed All or the most parte of his estate'.[15] In the Golden Valley there was little sympathy for Rowland.

Others less closely involved were also seeking retribution. Sir Arnold Herbert, the son of William Herbert of Oldcastle, who in 1595 had sold the Herbert's Dairies at Craswall to Rowland for £600, took him to court in 1619 for entering the property but only paying half its purchase price. Sir Arnold complained that Rowland 'being a verie polliticke gent' made excuses time and again for not producing written proof and craftily misleading him into thinking that he would make good the £300 shortfall. From late Elizabethan times the phrase 'politic gent' has been far from complimentary and Sir Arnold demanded his rights – either the full payment of £600 or surrender of the property, which now had a sale value of £1,000.[16]

The deals brokered in 1614-15 collapsed in 1621 when Rowland's brother Henry, having got his hands on the deeds of Wilmaston and other remaining property, expelled Rowland and Samuel West from them in order to transfer them to other trustees. West subsequently took Henry Vaughan to court but lost his case in 1622 'to the great prejudice and utter overthrow of Rowland Vaughan', who was forced into conveying Wilmaston and the lands in Turnastone,

Vowchurch and St Margaret's to Henry Vaughan's nominees, Howorth and Lake. Soon afterwards Henry Vaughan undertook Rowland's debts of £400 to James Rodd of Hereford and £1,600 to James Morgan as well as the ancient bond of £200 to William Vaughan.

Eventually the whole complicated tangle was simplified. New trustees, still including John Walcot, were appointed to put Wilmaston in trust for Henry in return for discharging more of Rowland's debts. Rowland conveyed some lands apparently part of the Wilmaston estate to Breinton, Morgan and a Mr Smith in trust for him at the yearly rent of £105, and finally he was given seven years in which to redeem the lands by paying off the debts. A similar arrangement was made for Rowland's various debts to other local creditors – Pennyman, Edward and James Husbands, Howorth and Lake, Pearle and Carwardine – all of whom were glad to extricate themselves.[17] Throughout, Henry was at the hub of the agreements, promising to give back to Rowland the deeds of his remaining lands, in return for which Henry would obtain the undisputed occupation of all the various premises upon entering into a bond for £1,000.

The trustees Walcot, Davies and Breinton were themselves hardly trustworthy. With some justification Rowland complained in 1623 that his creditors, his brother Henry, James Husbands and Roger Vaughan, had joined with Howorth and Rodd to set about felling woodland worth £200 'by reason thereof Rowland Vaughan after long imprisonment was forced to compound and agree with all the rest of his said creditors for their said debts for which he had formerly sold and conveyed most part of his lands'. Whether on this occasion imprisonment for debt is meant, or merely a loss of freedom to manage his personal affairs, is not clear. Howorth vigorously denied that trees had been felled except to repair houses already 'plucked down' by Rowland whose word, as Howorth put it, 'Being a man given to contention and suits of law', could not be trusted.[18]

However, as Rowland complained in 1621, the trustees had been receiving the Whitehouse rents for 12 years, amounting to £1,200, without the intention of paying him anything and refusing to deliver his lease. To this they calmly responded that there was no clause in the lease requiring them to do so. The Chancery courts were notorious for their slow procedures and Rowland was understandably dissatisfied. He brought a similar case early in 1625 but with differing evidence, still blaming Walcot for mishandling his London debts but now accusing all three trustees of having received the total huge sum of £3,000 in settlement of the original debt of a mere £365. They had, moreover, some years earlier persuaded Rowland's son Richard, who had since died, to part with his rights in Whitehouse as his mother's heir. Now, Rowland complained, they had 'confederated' with Epiphan Howorth, who 'lately hath pretended some estate ... to the Capital messuage and premises called the White House'.[19]

Epiphan and Blanche Howorth were understandably concerned about their inheritance of Whitehouse and although Rowland was still the legal occupant with his third wife, they were one step nearer its possession. Epiphan now took a further vital step by getting the trustees Walcot, Davies and Breinton to assign the remainder of the controversial 20-year lease to him, to which Rowland countered by attempting to cut Howorth out by settling the estate on Walcot. He failed, for Walcot then sold it to Howorth, who ejected Rowland 'since when his children have been destitute of anywhere to live'. Howorth commented that it had cost him almost its full value and he obtained the agreement of Rowland's daughters, Elizabeth and Katherine, 'cast off by their father without means or maintenance', by offering them out of his good intention as they were his wife's nieces, £400 'for their maintenance and portions towards their preferment in the way of marriage'.[20] At last he had wrested Rowland out of Whitehouse and had become its legal owner.

Meanwhile, a blow from another quarter was issued by Sir John Scudamore. One hour before sunset on the evening of Sunday 23 October 1623 Scudamore's two attorneys arrived at a house at Dore (which house is not known) to demand payment of Rowland's rent of £100 for the previous six months up to Michaelmas. The full procedure of the law was carried out. They were instructed to repeat the demand twice more before sunset and then, if not paid, formally take possession of the house and lands, finally requiring Rowland to shut the door on himself in the presence of four witnesses.[21]

By contrast, the family's ejection from Whitehouse was far less gentlemanly, being linked to a further lawsuit brought by Rowland in 1624-25. In this he made accusations that John Parry, William Beaver and Richard Arnold had been bribed by Howorth and Walcot to smash doors and windows at Whitehouse, expel Rowland, his wife and children, and break into closets and chests in order to take away all the deeds and writings they could find.[22] His complaint was a prelude to a longer dispute over rights of haymaking and harvesting on lands in Peterchurch, owned by Rowland but leased by Walcot to Parry. The evidence appears to reveal that Rowland and his evicted family had taken refuge with his father-in-law, as it was from the latter's alehouse

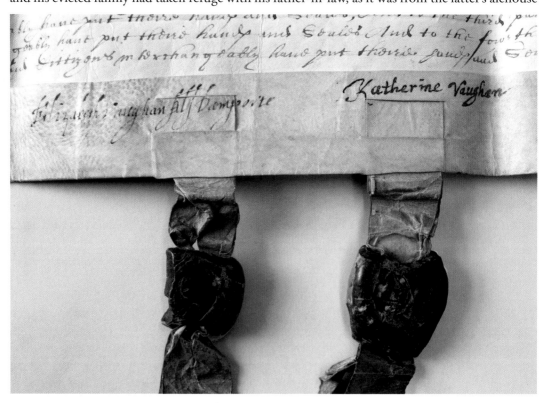

Fig. 8.1 The signatures of Rowland's two daughters,
Elizabeth and Katherine, on a sealed document in the Herefordshire Archive and Records Centre.
(HARC F37/9; thanks to Rhys Griffith for photography)

Fig. 8.2 Rowland's coat of arms in St Bartholomew's church, Vowchurch

that Rowland rallied Watkin Prosser, his wife's father, and Thomas Prosser, her uncle, to his support by cutting the barley and turning pigs and cattle into the disputed field. Walcot and Howorth called upon the county sheriff to have Rowland arrested. When they all arrived at Prosser's house a brawl broke out, with Rowland cursing and the womenfolk, Katherine Prosser and Anne Evans, joining in, one of whom got a black eye from Parry for her intervention.

This sorry episode is the last we hear of Rowland. He died at the age of 69 and his will was proved in 1627.[23] Unfortunately the will itself has not been located and there are no early surviving registers of the Golden Valley parishes that might have recorded his burial. His heirs, his son John and two daughters, Elizabeth and Katherine, formally broke their connections with the Poston and Whitehouse estates and other of their father's properties in 1629-30, transferring the Whitehouse estate to Epiphan Howorth.[24] By November of that year his daughter Elizabeth had evidently married, as her surname was recorded as Damporte or Davenporte but no further trace of the lives of any of Rowland's three heirs has been found.[25] The Whitehouse estate remained in the possession of Epiphan Howorth's descendants until 1981.

Rowland's coat of arms (Fig. 8.2), with the carved legend 'RV 1613', is fixed with other armorials in the church nave at Vowchurch (although incorrectly displayed).[26] No portrait or memorial of Rowland has been found. He was, however, remembered by his last wife Elizabeth who, after Rowland's death, married Richard Leighton, a relative of John Parry of Poston. Her crudely carved and spelled slab monument is mounted on the vestry wall at Peterchurch. It reads:

```
1640


        †
       IHS


HEERE  LYETHE  T
HE  THE  BODY  OF
ELIZA  LEYGHTON
WYFE  TO  RICH
LEYGH  GEN[TLEM]AN
FORMERLY  MAR
IED  ROVLAND
VAVGHAN  ES
QR  DECEASED
```

Fig. 8.3 Transcript of monument in Peterchurch
vestry to Elizabeth Leyghton, previously
Rowland's third wife.

9   EXPLORING THE RELICS

The evidence for Rowland Vaughan's 16th-century waterworks has been eroded over time by a range of natural processes resulting in loose, mixed deposits ('colluvium') overlaying the valley floor as it existed at the time of his original water management schemes. These deposits have been often formed at the break of slope where the adjacent upland slopes and the valley floor margins meet, as a result of sheet wash erosion on the adjacent slopes or farming practices on the valley floor. Structural features for diverting the water from the rivers to the irrigation channels such as sluices and weirs may have been partially lost through lack of maintenance and later alterations. The evidence for irrigation and drainage channels may also have been destroyed by changes in land use which have resulted in the ploughing up of former areas of water-meadows; or where former ridge and furrow bedworks (channels used to distribute water over the flat plain, see Chapter 3) were levelled so that modern farm machinery could be used to cut the hay crop. It is also important to distinguish between the irrigation and drainage channels developed as part of the Rowland Vaughan waterworks system and the later developments which sought to improve the drainage in fields as part of 19th-century agricultural improvement schemes.

However, there are significant features of the waterworks remaining in the landscape in that part of the valley mainly to the west of the river Dore, where water has been diverted from the western tributaries of the river over terraces to flow into the Trench Royal at Poston; and the bedworks fed by the Slough brook at Turnastone to form part of a managed irrigation and flood control system on the adjacent slopes. In addition, in the valley floor east of the Trench Royal and extending to the Dore south of Poston Court to Turnastone are the fragmented remnants of a bedwork system.

Our surveys have sought to distinguish these features using a range of techniques including field surveys supplemented with a photographic record of important features, including aerial photographs and LIDAR images. We have reconstructed the main elements of the system in a series of maps and other documentary evidence, to interpret how the system was managed and its main agricultural benefits in regulating water flows in the valley.

The main components of the waterworks in the Golden Valley
In this chapter the focus is on the second stage of his scheme between Peterchurch and Turnastone and the third stage between the Slough brook and Turnastone. These were developed after the acquisition of the Whitehouse estate through his second marriage, and by securing leases over the lands at Poston Court between Turnastone and Peterchurch in the early 1600s.

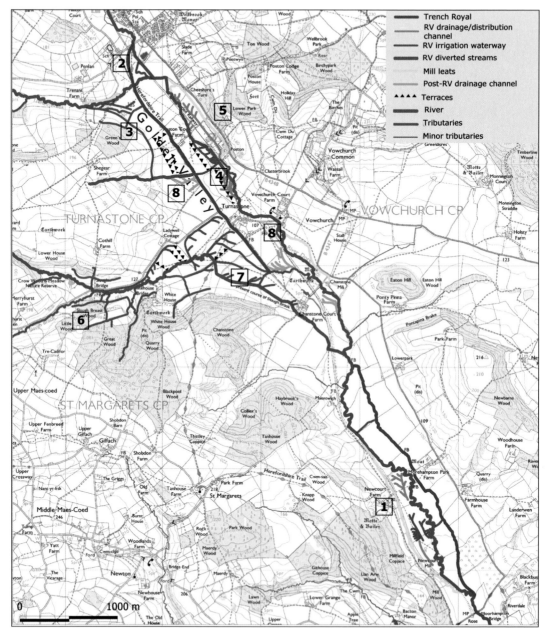

Map 9.1 *Landscape features of Rowland's (RV) waterworks in the Golden Valley.*
The boxed numbers on the map are referenced in the text.
(© Crown copyright 2016 OS Licence No.100057492)

The field surveys carried out by the Golden Valley Study Group (GVSG) over the last 15 years, themselves based on the framework developed by Penelope Wood and described in Chapter 6, have been overlaid onto the Ordnance Survey map of the Golden Valley to produce Map 9.1. This illustrates the complexity of the scheme and shows how the remnants in the landscape today provide evidence for several different types of water-meadow features.

The field surveys define the components and the extent of the integrated system of artificial canals, sluices, weirs and distribution channels and their role in the management of water-meadows in the Golden Valley. They also highlight the relationship to the river Dore and its tributaries and the development of catchworks (channels used to divert water along the valley sides) in the upper Slough valley and a hybrid form of bedworks in the wider, flatter valley floor in the Newcourt, Turnastone and Poston Court farm meadows.

Some of the evidence for Rowland's original waterworks along the valley floor has been lost to subsequent changes in farming practices and land use, with the extension of arable farming in the Second World War to increase food production, and subsequent changes to adapt to globalisation in the first part of the 21st century. However, additional water-meadow features have been identified with the aid of LIDAR which has also enabled the verification or adjustment of elements identified in the field surveys. Map 9.1 also identifies other features in the landscape that may represent parts of the original system. The numbered locations on the map are cross-referenced in the following text.

The second stage of Rowland's waterworks from Peterchurch to Turnastone
The passage of the water captured from the natural watercourses by Rowland in his waterworks can be divided into three stages:
>   1. The water from springs and streams which feed the brooks;
>   2. Between the brooks and the Trench Royal;
>   3. From the Trench Royal into the river Dore.

The layout of the waterworks follows a repeating pattern all the way down the valley from Peterchurch to Bacton. Water from a brook or spring is diverted into channels on the contour so as to 'drown' land above the Trench Royal. The diverted channel then flows into the next watercourse, which then drains it into the river or into the Trench Royal. In its first section the Trench Royal acts as a drain to the meadows on the west bank. However, below Poston Court, the Trench Royal becomes both 'master' and 'servant', draining the west bank and by way of sluice gates supplying a steady flow of water to meadows on the east (see No.5 on Map 9.1) where there is a complex system of terraces and bedworks along which the water flows before eventually draining back into the river Dore.

Relationships between the Trench Royal and the river Dore (No.2 on Map 9.1).
The original course of the river Dore has been severely disrupted since Rowland's day by the building of the Golden Valley Railway in the 1870s, the remnants of which follow the northern field boundary. The diversion of the river by the railway has resulted in the straightening of the river course and the isolation of the old course in several places down the Golden Valley (see Map 9.1 and Fig. 9.2). In Fig.9.1 the old course of the river Dore is still evident after winter rains which collect in the old channel.

Fig. 9.1 Remnants of the river Dore in 'Upper Weir Meadow' (No.2 on Map 9.1)

This is also mirrored in the old course of the Trench Royal (see Fig. 9.2), which started at Horsepool bridge in Peterchurch and flowed across Upper Weir Meadow from the northern corner to the south corner where it meets the Trenant brook. This section was controlled by a series of sluices and weirs. The details are more evident in the LIDAR Tile for this area (Fig. 9.3).

Fig. 9.2 Aerial photo of the source of the Trench Royal at Peterchurch

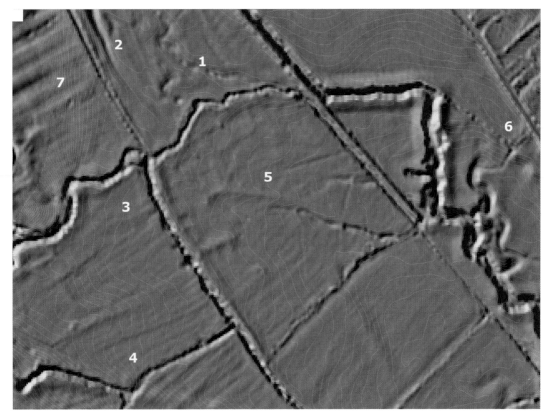

Fig 9.3 LIDAR image showing origins of Trench Royal – below Horsepool Bridge
1. *Dry channel of diverted river Dore subsequent to the Golden Valley Railway.*
2. *Dry channel of Trench Royal from weir and sluice on river Dore at Horsepool bridge.*
3. *Weir and sluice diverting Trenant brook into Trench Royal and diverted Trenant draining back to river Dore.*
4. *Irrigation channels from Trenant Brook to Trench Royal.*
5. *Dry channel of Trenant draining land between Trench Royal and river Dore.*
6. *Weir and mill leat leading to Poston Mill and second weir and return channel to river Dore to control water levels on mill leat at Poston.*
7. *Remnants of ridge and furrow medieval plough land.*

The flow of the Trench Royal in the Upper Weir Meadow/Upper Langford field was controlled by a sluice. The evidence from LIDAR (Fig 9.3, Nos. 1-5) shows that the Trenant brook was diverted by a sluice and weir before following a diverted channel back to the river Dore (see section below on 'Evidence in the landscape for the weirs and sluices today'). The old channel is evident, flowing across the field below its present course. Upstream, the Trenant is diverted to flow in an east/west direction back to the Trench Royal. To the north of the system, on the edge of Peterchurch, is a field with remnants of ridge and furrow medieval ploughland which have been eroded by subsequent cultivation (Fig. 9.3, No.7).

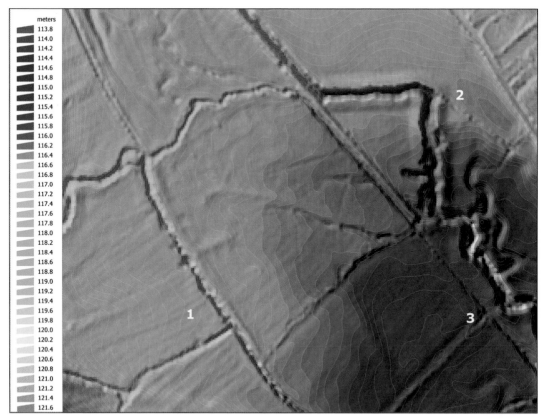

Fig 9.4 LIDAR image showing origins of Poston Mill leat / source of waterworks – flood plain between Trench Royal and river Dore.
1. Straight course of the Trench Royal possibly following the course of a secondary Roman track running north of the Trenant brook weir and sluice.
2. The meandering course of the river Dore draining its natural flood-plain, the line of the Golden Valley Railway and origins of the Poston Mill leat.
3. Colour-coded gradient of flood-plain with low point in south east corner (fall from 118m to 114m).

In Fig. 9.4 the straight line of the Trench Royal (No.1) shows clearly, possibly following the course of the minor Roman track running north and south along the valley. According to this theory, held by a number of people locally, the second stage of Rowland's scheme may have occurred to him when, on one day of floods, he noticed water from the Trenant brook in spate flowing into one of the ditches beside the Roman road, and following it until it joined the Shegear brook to flow back into the Dore. Supporting this theory is the observation that the canal flows in a cutting through a slight rise in the land in order to keep its straight course as it approaches Turnastone, instead of deviating to follow a more natural lower course to the west.

By contrast, the meandering course of the river Dore flows erratically over its natural flood-plain, which has been bisected by the straight-lined Golden Valley Railway and by modern field boundaries (Figs. 9.4 & 9.5). The colour-coded gradient of the flood-plain shows a fall from 118m in the north-west to a low point of 114m in the south-east corner of Upper Weir

Meadow. The evidence for Rowland's waterworks in the land between the Trench Royal and the river Dore in this section has been eroded by later cultivation.

The Trenant/Shegear brook catchworks & hybrid bedworks (No.3 on Map 9.1)
The most upstream example of the diversion of brooks flowing from the adjacent uplands to the west of the river Dore is where the waters of the Trenant brook are diverted by a weir and sluice above Trenant farm which raises the water into a large trench on the opposite bank to the farm (see channels identified as No.3 on Map 9.1). This flows into a channel which follows the contour below Green's Wood (see Figs. 9.5 & 9.6) until it joins the upper part of the Shegear brook, which was diverted to join the Trench Royal. A major sluice and weir then diverts it to link up with the river Dore (see section below on 'Evidence in the landscape for the weirs and sluices today').

Fig. 9.5 Channel linking Trenant-Shegear catchworks running below Green's Wood

Fig. 9.6 Terraces and hybrid bedworks between the Trenant and Shegear brooks above Poston Court (No.3 on Map 9.1)

Fig. 9.7 Fields and terraces above Poston Court

Ridges and terraces to control the flow of water across the land can be clearly seen looking up-slope from the Trench Royal near Poston Court Farm (No.3 on Map 9.1 and Figs. 9.6-9.7). These terraces enabled the water to be managed so that it flowed in an even sheet across the land. Rowland's waterworks captured these streams and distributed their waters over the valley floor before draining into the Trench Royal.

Figs 9.6 and 9.7 show the following features:

1. The valley floor running north/south at 120m below the adjacent uplands which rise to 250-300m above sea level, and to over 600m in the Black Mountains to the west.

2. That the juncture between the adjacent limestone outcrops and the valley floor terraces is particularly marked where smaller streams and springs have eroded into the limestone.

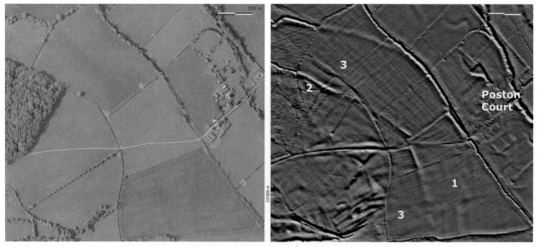

Fig. 9.8 LIDAR image of terraces and hybrid bedworks between the Trenant and Shegear brooks above Poston Court (No.3 on Map 9.1).
1. Terraces for spreading irrigation water from catchworks between Trenant and Shegear brooks to form hybrid bedworks.
2. Extensive ridge and furrow cultivation in what is now Green's wood.
3. The catchworks channel linking the Trenant brook and the Shegear brook above Poston Court Farm.

3. The horizontal lines (now often bounded by hedgerows) which mark the irrigation channels from the Trenant brook at the foot of the limestone slopes, and the line of the Trench Royal between the Trenant and the Dore. These features and the retaining terraces can be clearly seen on the LIDAR image for this area (Fig. 9.8). The crop marks of spring-sown wheat in the field on the left of Fig. 9.7 show these terraces clearly. It is possible that the terraces represent remnants of former river terraces of the Dore as it moved across its flood plain, and that they have been enhanced by using the material excavated from the trenches to form the major irrigation channels.

The lines of the retaining terraces are particularly marked and cross the former line of the Shegear brook, suggesting that this was part of Rowland's original waterworks. The water which followed the old Shegear brook flowed into the river Dore via a weir and sluice on the Shegear which flooded the fields between the Shegear brook at Poston Court and Turnastone Court.

The terraces, drainage and irrigation channels forming bedworks south of Poston Court to Turnastone (No.4 on Map 9.1)

The aerial photograph and LIDAR image in Fig. 9.9 show that in this section of Rowland's waterworks the evidence for bedworks, distribution channels and terraces is still evident in the landscape (see (a) and (b) on LIDAR image). Banks and terraces to control the flow can be clearly seen in Turnastone Meadow, as well as the place where the floodwater drained back into the river (Fig. 9.10).

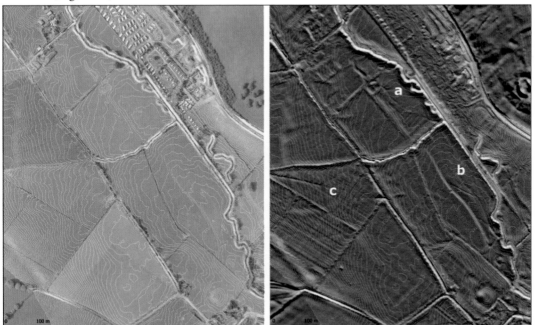

Fig. 9.9 Waterworks between Poston Court and Turnastone Court Farm:
matched aerial photo and LIDAR scan.
a) Bedworks between Poston Court and Shegear brook
b) Turnastone Meadow south of Poston Court
c) Post-Rowland Vaughan channels south of Shegear brook

Fig. 9.10 Bedworks in meadow south of Poston Court (No.4 on Map 9.1)

Members of the GVSG accompanied Katherine Stearne, who has written extensively on the identification and operation of water-meadows, on a field walk[1] and it was confirmed that there were remnants of bedworks in this part of the Golden Valley. In Fig. 9.10 the bedworks follow a ridge and furrow pattern, but with the distance between the channels larger than the average for ridge and furrow (11ft), identified by Skelton (see Chapter 3).

In Fig. 9.11 the features in Turnastone Meadow on the south side of the Shegear brook are very well marked in this early spring scene after a dry period. The photograph looks north-west

Fig. 9.11 Distribution, drainage channels and spreading terrace in Turnastone Meadow
(No.4 on Map 9.1) south of Poston Court

across the field and identifies the spreading terrace as a raised straight line, just below the hedge line (No.1 on Fig. 9.11).

The curved drainage channel takes water off a now derelict sluice gate on the Shegear brook and returns the water to the river Dore via a long drainage channel (No.2 on Fig. 9.11). However, in Katherine Stearne's view the more common feature of water-meadow management in the Rowland system was more closely related to a form of 'basin irrigation'.[2] These are wide plains where water was let in for short periods, leaving the silt to settle before draining away. Rowland constantly emphasised the benefits from 'muddy fluds' spreading across the land and fertilising the soil. Letting water settle to deposit the silts and calcareous minerals would have been an important feature of his system.

In this part of the system, the distribution and drainage channels are well developed and form a hybrid form of bedworks. The earthworks comprise a large drain, 0.6m deep, fed by a network of lesser ditches which join it in a curved, herringbone fashion. Because these do not form straight drainage channels it is unlikely that they post-date Rowland's waterworks, although they could have been subject to later modification, and Nicky Smith[3] has suggested they may be of more recent origin.

In Fig. 9.12 the natural flood meadow north of the bridge at Vowchurch illustrates the rich diversity of heavy cropping grasses, which benefit from the natural siltation from winter flooding. In this case, the water flows were not systematically managed, but the shallow hollow in the centre of the field, where the water was allowed to settle, has developed a heavy hay crop. Rowland, recognised these natural features and introduced a system of weirs, sluice and drainage channels to control the flow of water to create these natural basins, and encouraged them to drain in the winter and to flood the meadows in the spring and summer with a moving film of water.

Fig. 9.12 Flood meadow by the river Dore at Vowchurch – Bridge Field, south of Turnastone Court Farm. The line of trees indicates the course of the river.

The third stage of Rowland's waterworks
from the upper Slough brook to Turnastone meadows

The upper Slough brook catchworks (No. 6 on Map 9.1)

On the slopes above the main brooks there is a complex catchwork of channels carrying water from springs and minor brooks to irrigate sloping fields. One such channel can be seen behind the seat on the Crow Wood nature reserve ('a' on Map 9.2). Starting at the source in Crow Wood, water was collected from springs into small channels which led slightly downhill along the contour line, from where it flowed down across sloping fields and drained into brooks.

Field evidence on the nature reserve shows a small channel which can still be seen behind the seat at the top of the slope below the area of 'wood-pasture'. Water distributed along this channel flowed down across the meadow (now covered with ant-heaps – 'ant-i-tumps' – indicating land which has not been ploughed for many years) and joined the ditch from the spring below Cothill to drain into the Dolward brook. The springs which fed this channel now only flow in times of flood. The field names are identified in Map 9.2. There is also a channel carrying water from this spring which runs along above the field now planted as a vineyard, defining the upper boundary of the field. Further along, the water drained down natural channels into the Slough brook.

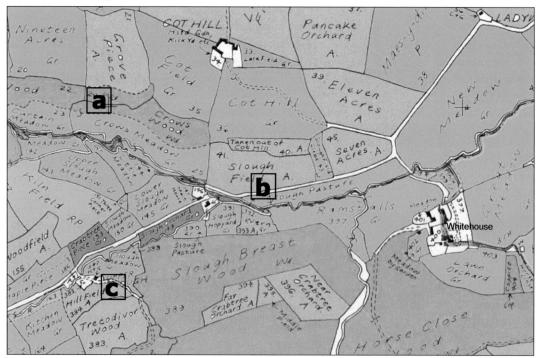

Map 9.2 Upper Slough brook field names and land use – 1842-43 tithe map
a) Crow wood catchworks
b) Slough brook cliff
c) New Pasture grist mill
(for key to land use colour coding see Map 3.7, page 37)

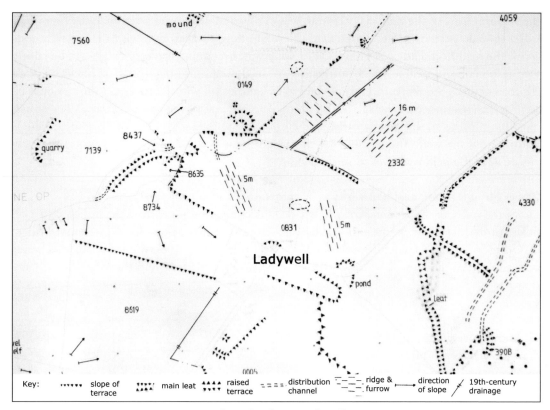

Map 9.3 Catchworks above Ladywell, Turnastone.
(Skelton, Golden Valley Archaeological Survey)[4]

Other channels can be seen above Ladywell (Map 9.3). Here a now-dry spring fed a former brook, which was diverted towards the flood-plain via a complex system of collecting channels eventually to irrigate the area above the Trench Royal between the Trenant brook and the Slough brook. Another perennial spring close by is located south-west of the footpath which leads up from Slough Bridge to Cothill.

Tufa is precipitated out of the overflow water from this spring as it runs down the ditch already mentioned. Until recently the water was pumped up to Cothill Farm from this spring by means of a hydraulic ram – a wonderfully simple device, which gets its energy from the natural flow in a watercourse.

Downstream from the boundary between Slough Hopyard and Wern Pasture the brook has changed course, taking a sharp turn against a low earth cliff ((b) on Map 9.2). When the early 20th-century large-scale Ordnance Survey map was made, this sharp turn was shown just downstream of the boundary. It has eroded to its present position over the course of a hundred years. At the base of the cliff a deposit of peat can be seen, laid down when the valley was under a lake held back in ice-age times by a moraine. Twigs and leaves can be seen, having been perfectly preserved for thousands of years in the anaerobic peat.

A short distance further downstream a 90cm high by 8cm thick oak post sticks up from the bed of the stream. The post is probably morticed into an oak sill embedded in the bed of the stream – part of the remains of a weir, which diverted water into a channel carrying water half a mile downstream to the large field (New Meadow on Map 9.2) with the big redwoods across the road from Ladywell House. Three long water-retaining banks or ridges can be faintly seen (especially noticeable when buttercups are in flower), running across this field between the road and the brook. As recently as the 1990s another sill with mortices cut into it could be seen in the stream-bed at the site of the sluice. This has since been washed away. A few stones remaining in the stream-bank on the side closest to the road show the location of the sluice leading from the weir. The channel which carried the water to New Meadow was still clearly visible until the field was levelled in the 1990s.

Lower Slough brook and bedworks at Turnastone (No.7 on Map 9.1)
Down the valley of the Slough brook weirs and sluices diverted water from the brook onto level fields on both sides of the brook. There was a large weir just below the Whitehouse bridge, diverting water onto land below the house. From this weir a sinuous channel carried water across 'New Meadow', which adjoins the road between Turnastone and the Whitehouse Gate (known as 'Red Gate', but now white). This can be seen from the road.

Another weir is located further down, where a footbridge carries the footpath from Ladywell to Turnastone across the brook. Here an enormous stone slab (Fig. 9.13), standing up in the bed of the brook, formed part of the weir. Another part is built of stonework, which is partly concealed among bushes and brambles.

Fig. 9.13 Stone slab weir diverting the Slough brook

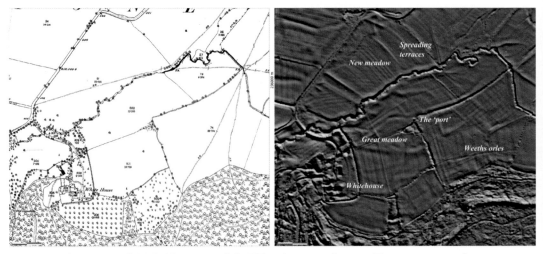

Fig. 9.14 LIDAR image of the Whitehouse and upper Turnastone meadows

At the 'sheep wash' the Slough brook is joined by a canal from a 'port' below the Whitehouse (Fig. 9.14) from where small punts or barges could transport people and goods along the diverted Slough brook, past Chanstone and then via the river – held back by a weir – and along the Trench Royal as far as Newcourt. Rowland claimed[5] that all kind of goods – soil, stone, manure, compost and hay, as well as people – could be transported around the estate by boat. There are further ridges and drainage channels in the part of the field towards The Cross House at Turnastone.

The downstream end of this part of the Trench Royal connects with another earlier course of the Slough brook, which carried the water from the Trench Royal back to the river. Between the end of the Trench Royal and the river Dore, the former Slough brook carried a series of braided drainage channels which drained back to the river (No.8 on Map 9.1, page 94), but they are considered to be later than Rowland because the channels are too straight. In Rowland's system, the channels always followed a slight curve to slow down the rate at which the water drained down the channel in order to spread the water across the land.

Further on, the Slough brook is diverted from its original course towards Turnastone at the 'sheep wash', and led via a small canal along the edge of the level land towards Chanstone Court (Fig. 9.15). There are still sluices along this stretch of the brook, which released water onto fields between the canal and the Trench Royal, marking the third stage of the system noted on p.104. The spread bank running diagonally from the sluice may have carried water onto the meadow or separated two areas of irrigation.

In the aerial photograph (Fig. 9.15) it is evident that the Slough brook was diverted further south from its original course on the lower reaches of the Trench Royal so as to enclose a greater extent of flat-bottomed land between it and the river at Turnastone. In this system, a

Fig. 9.15 Aerial photograph of fields west of Turnastone

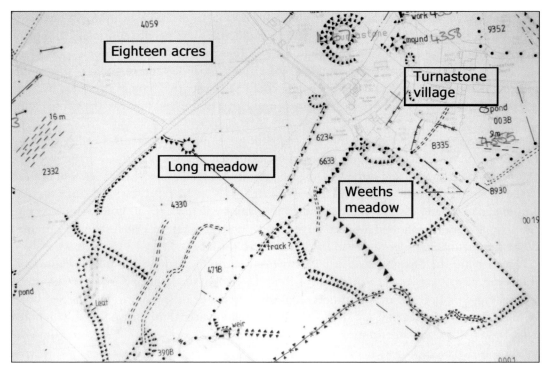

*Map 9.4 Lower Slough brook and Turnastone meadows. For key to symbols see Map 9.3, page 105.
(Skelton, Golden Valley Archaeological Survey)*

weir and sluice diverted water from the brook into a channel which led down the valley to feed a hybrid bedwork system at Turnastone. It is likely that an earlier course of the Slough brook led to Turnastone near The Cross House. A winding hedge follows a trench as far as the Trench Royal, and then skirts the garden of Turnastone shop. The Slough brook in flood still follows this course, and can even flow down the road past the shop. Perhaps this was the original most direct course of the brook back to the river, which was diverted to keep it clear of the village.

These changes in drainage channels and the terraces to spread the water over the Turnastone meadows are defined below in Map 9.4 and also highlighted in the LIDAR image (Fig. 9.16), which illustrate how another weir and sluice in the brook near the Whitehouse diverted water on to the land below the house and was spread over levelled platforms by a series of terraces and irrigation channels.

In Fig. 9.16 the contours and colour gradation show clearly how the land slopes in a south-easterly direction between the adjacent uplands, the Trench Royal and the river Dore. This area was also surveyed by English Heritage in 2003-04[6] and their survey plan for the lower Turnastone meadows shows that the Long Meadow and Weeths Meadow are covered with minor water channels and linear depressions, no more than 0.5m wide and 0.2m deep. They run parallel to each other and are spaced between about 10 to 15m apart. They do not have the usual undulating form of ridge and furrow cultivation, but appear as narrow cuts in the ground surface. The English Heritage study concluded that they were neither plough marks nor parallel drains, which were widely laid out in the late 19th century to improve drainage. The study concluded that:

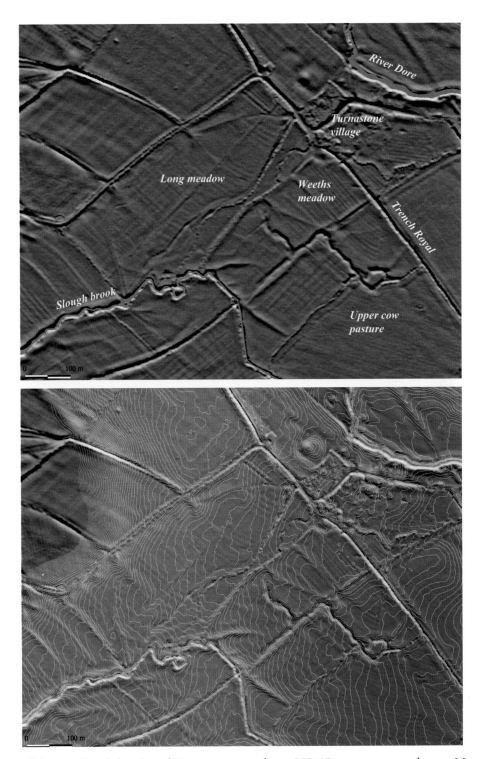

Fig. 9.16 Lower Slough brook and Turnastone meadows. LIDAR scan corresponding to Map 9.4 and the same view with contour shading.

Water may have been carried across the meadow by these ditches and by channels, which overflowed into basins to be retained by (former field) banks on one side, while on the other side it may have flowed back into ditches or towards banks, which diverted it back into the main watercourse.

This integrated system needed careful management to operate efficiently and take account of the different weather conditions to prevent storm waters destroying weirs, sluices and trenches. The archives of the Whitehouse estate show that a lease in 1796 required the landlord to erect floodgates, which were also identified as landmarks for defining the manorial boundary of Snodhill in 1824, both of which suggest that the sluices on the Slough brook and the sheep-wash on the meadows below Whitehouse remained in use. Members of the Wood family, who owned the Whitehouse estate, have also suggested that the estate maintained these systems until late in the 19th or early 20th centuries. [7]

Other features in the landscape that may represent parts of the original system

Post-Rowland Vaughan irrigation channels (No.8 on Map 9.1)

The field below Green's Wood, covered in buttercups (a marker for former water-meadows), shows signs of possible drainage channels obscured by later cultivation. However, a conversation with Mr James of Poston Court Farm indicated that these resulted from 19th-century horse-drawn ploughs which left the distinctive plough lines or 'rhines' evident in the photograph below. The LIDAR images for this part of the scheme also show evidence for extensive ridge and furrow cultivation in what is now Green's Wood and in fields adjacent to the upper Trenant brook (see Fig. 9.8).

Today, the water coming down the brook, combined with that brought from the Trenant by the channel, is diverted into a further channel which branches out across a field (Fig. 9.18),

Fig. 9.17 Field below Green's Wood (No.8 on Map 9.1, page 94) –
19th-century horse plough lines or 'rhines' running down the hill slope

Fig. 9.18 Post-Rowland irrigation channels (No.8 on Map 9.1, page 94)

creating a marshy place just short of the Trench Royal. These channels, unlike those created by Rowland, are straight and right-angled compared to the curved channels used by Rowland to reduce the rate of flow (see green crop-marks in Fig. 9.19).

The braided channels and later drainage channels defined by their straight lines and rectangular features are clearly defined on the aerial photograph (Fig. 9.8) and in Figs 9.18 and 9.19 which show distribution channels as water-filled, straight-lined channels in winter and as crop-marks in early spring growth.

Fig. 9.19 Post-Rowland channels (No.8 on Map 9.1, page 94)

Fig. 9.20 Post-Rowland 'drainage' using diverted course of Shegear brook near Poston Court (No.8 on Map 9.1, page 94)

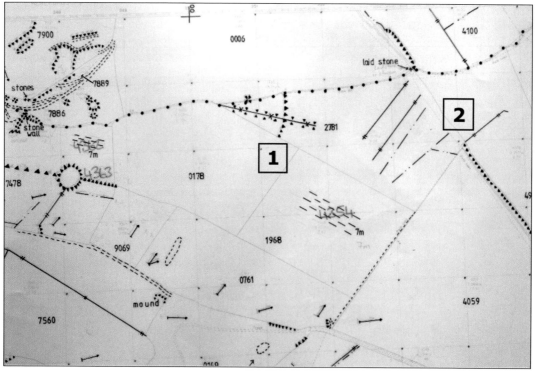

Map 9.5 Drainage patterns below Shegear brook. For key to symbols see Map 9.3, page 105. (Skelton, Golden Valley Archaeological Survey)

The intense green of the grass in early growth in Fig. 9.19 illustrates the veracity of Rowland's claim in *His Booke* that where moles create leakages in mill leats and streams, the early spring watering of the meadows will bring forward an 'early bite'. It is possible that in Rowland's original scheme the water fed into the next section of the Trench Royal (see Fig. 9.20). The field was extensively cultivated during the Second World War and it is unlikely that any evidence for Rowland's original waterworks in this field has survived.

Between the place where the water was diverted into the channel across the field and the weirs on the Trench Royal the former bed of the stream was filled in, but it can be seen meandering across the landscape south-west of the straightened Shegear brook.

The survey maps in the Skelton report confirm these features (Nos.1 & 2 on Map 9.5), which identified an additional terrace which spread the water across the field. These features are also evident in the LIDAR image (Fig. 9.9). The map also shows the more recent parallel drainage channels to the Trench Royal, which is dry today in this section (as indicated by the gap in the tooth-marked line of the Trench Royal (see No.2 on Map 9.5).

Watermills and Waterworks

From the examples at Newcourt and Poston it is apparent that another important influence on the development of water management systems was the diversion of water along mill leats and its return via mill tails to the river source, with a ponded reservoir to balance the flows. The Golden Valley Archaeological Survey[8] also studied the remnants of water use in the Golden Valley between Dorstone and Chanstone (see Map 9.8). This map identified the extensive leats and weirs associated with the Trenant, Poston Court and Chanstone mills. In addition, there is also evidence for watermills at Newcourt, Morehampton and Abbeydore (see Chapter 4).

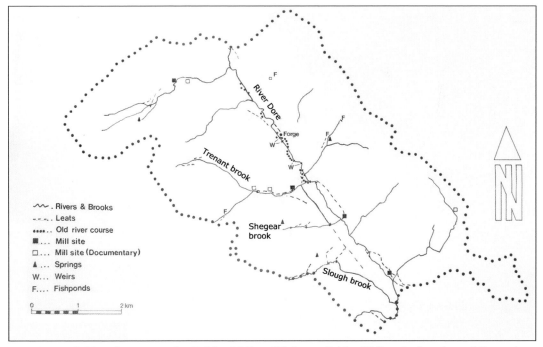

Map 9.6 Use of water in the Golden Valley. (Skelton, Golden Valley Archaeological Survey)

There is therefore a significant association between the distribution of watermills and the development of Rowland's water management system (see Maps 9.6 and 9.7). This type of technology for transferring water flows over considerable distance could be readily adapted to the management of irrigation systems, and the innovations developed by Rowland enabled the flow of water across the meadows to be managed and drained.

G. Atwood[9] has argued that the origins of systems more sophisticated than 'floating upwards' may be observed in the juxtaposition of mill streams (taking water to mills at a high level) and mill tails (taking water at a lower level). Leakages from the mill leats into the fields below may also have suggested an approach to more formal methods of irrigation and the spread of water. We have already noted the possibility that Rowland was influenced by this relationship at Newcourt, where he noted how water leaking from streams and the leat leading to an overshot mill had enhanced the growth of grass below. The development of his overall scheme in the Golden Valley shows a close relationship between irrigation channels, drainage and mill leats for the integrated management of the river Dore.

Map 9.7 shows the relationship between land ownership and watermills between Peterchurch and Chanstone. Their distribution on the tributary streams and the river Dore is associated with different types of water-meadow management. To the west of the river Dore, the mill leats on the Trenant ((a) on Map 9.7) and the upper part of the Slough brook ((b) on Map 9.7) were

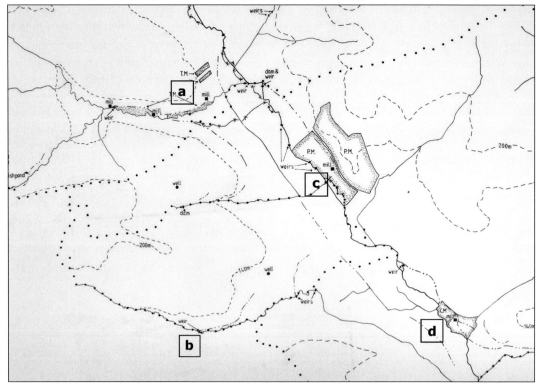

Map 9.7 Watermills between Peterchurch and Chanstone with stippled areas showing the land belonging to the mills. (Skelton, Golden Valley Archaeological Survey)
a) Trenant Mill   b) Upper Slough brook grist mill
c) Poston Mill   d) Chanstone Mill

used in connection with catchwork schemes. The land to the east of the river Dore and the mill leat at Poston were associated with drainage/irrigation schemes to form hybrid bedwork schemes ((c) on Map 9.7) and (No.5 on Map 9.1).

Fig. 9.21 Three-way sluice controlling water channels from the Trenant Mill

Fig. 9.22 The weir on the Trenant brook

The Trenant Mill ('a' on Map 9.7)

The Trenant Mill was situated downstream from Trenant farm and was fed by a leat taking water from a weir on the Trenant brook. The land belonging to the mill was about 9 acres between the leat and the brook. The mill was still standing until the mid-1970s, when it was demolished because it was unsafe. The evidence for the sluice and weir can still be seen in the landscape today (Figs 9.21 and 9.22).

The Skelton report identifies this mill as one of three mills on the Trenant brook which were shown on Taylor's map (1786)[10] as the 'Urishay Mills'. One of these mills lies further upstream and the other may have been to the west of Trenant farm, but little evidence is left today.

The weir and sluice above Trenant farm raise the water into a large trench on the opposite bank to the farm (No.3 on Map 9.1, page 94). This flows into a channel which follows the contour below Green's Wood and feeds a series of channels flowing across the fields which slope towards the Trench Royal.

Description of the Slough valley watermills ('b' on Map 9.7)

In the valley of the Slough brook there are also two fair-sized trenches approximately 2m wide which not only served as 'drowning' courses but also as leats or mill races. A substantial mill-leat to feed the 'Wern Pasture' grist-mill collected water from a weir further upstream on the Slough brook ('b' on Map 9.7).

This led the water above the fields called Slough Forge Orchard and Slough Hopyard, defining the lower edge of Slough Breast Wood (Map 9.2). Along the leat, water from the brook is augmented by two springs in the wood, one a very strong one and the other seasonal. The leat then leads into the sloping field known as Wern Pasture, where it is enlarged into a long 'holding-pond' retained by a dam on the downhill side.

Fig. 9.23 Mill leat and pond for upper Slough brook mill

This pond may have fed into a second in the dingle below, which has a raised rim to give it more capacity, so providing a good head of water for powering the mill at the foot of the dingle. A channel from the opposite direction around a spur of the land feeds into the holding-pond, bringing more water from springs in the Great Wood on the other side of the hill. This channel is very faint and hard to see on the ground, but it is clearly visible from the road below in low evening sunlight, or when winter sun melts frost along its bank. The downhill bank can also be traced in late summer, when small yellow hawkweed – which thrives on subsoil – grows on the excavated material.

There is possibly another mill-pond and grist-mill where the channel from the Great Wood levels out and changes direction before descending and rounding the spur. The pond can be seen, and there is stonework in the gulley below it suggesting a mounting for a mill-wheel. Sometime in the 20th century the tenant farmer cut a channel through the earth bank to drain the 'untidy' pond – since when it has been dry.

The drainage channels between the mill-leat to Poston Mill and the river Dore ('c' on Map 9.7 and No.5 on Map 9.1)

The mill at Poston was served by a 920m-long leat from the river Dore at the parish boundary with Peterchurch and the leat is well defined in the field today. The mill had a 4.3m overshot wheel and in the Tithe Apportionment of 1845, the land belonging to Poston Mill was 67 acres. On this land there is evidence for an extensive system of drainage/irrigation channels running from north-west to south-east and fed by waters leading from the mill leat and weirs on the river Dore with a main drainage channel back into the river Dore. Since Penelope Wood identified a series of drainage and distribution channels on her map, the visual evidence for

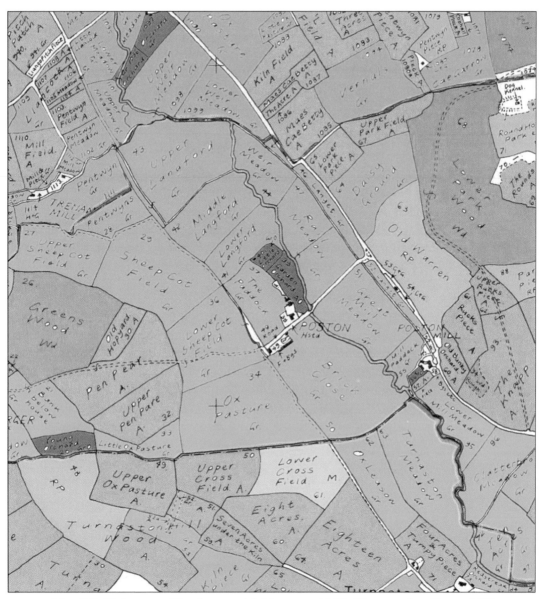

Map 9.8 Tithe map of land use and field names, 1842-45, centred on Poston Mill.
(For key to land use colour coding see Map 3.7, page 37)

the channels has been eroded by subsequent farming practice. However, the field names on the tithe maps 1842-45 indicate that the fields were known as meadows – Weir Meadow, Rail Meadow and Great Mill Meadow (Map 9.8).

In the case of land owned by Chanstone Mill ('d' on Map 9.7), the area is much smaller (12.5 acres); the drainage channels run south of the land owned by the mill and are straighter than those associated with Rowland's schemes and were probably developed independently (see No.8 on Map 9.1, page 94).

Evidence in the landscape for the weirs and sluices today

The weirs and sluices which diverted the river flows have been largely ruined through neglect and later alterations. However, R.E. Kay[11] has provided detailed diagrams for the sites of weir and sluice gates for the beginnings of the system south of Peterchurch and at Poston Court Farm on the river Dore, and for the upper and lower reaches of Slough brook. He was able to document the surviving structures in the late 1960s and early 1970s, when the original arrangements seemed to be reasonably clear. Our subsequent surveys have documented the remains as they are today.

Weirs and sluice gates diverting water from the Trenant brook into the Trench Royal

Kay first identified the weirs which diverted the Trenant brook into the head of the Trench Royal, which consisted of two weirs and complementary sluice gates – one for controlling water flows into the Trench Royal, and the other across the brook itself. This diverted the old course of the stream to form an overspill. The latter blocking weir was no longer in place when he carried out his survey, but the site was marked by three large sandstone slabs which spanned the existing overspill channel (Fig. 9.24 a).

The secondary weir has also been destroyed and was marked by a portion of its 'pitched stone turbulence platform' in the bed of the stream which still flowed into the Trench Royal. These platforms had an important function to minimise the undercutting of the weir foundation and side banks of the channel below from the turbulence of the water passing over the weir itself. They usually had retaining walls on either side and Kay has noted that evidence for these retaining walls on the west and east side of the channel could still be seen in the pitched stone area. There was a concrete arched platform of recent construction which probably formed

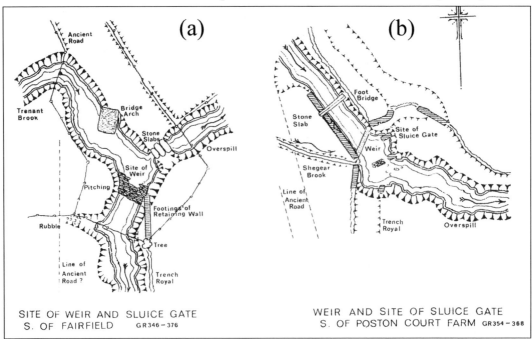

SITE OF WEIR AND SLUICE GATE
S. OF FAIRFIELD GR346-376

WEIR AND SITE OF SLUICE GATE
S. OF POSTON COURT FARM GR354-368

Fig. 9.24 Drawings of weirs and sluices on the river Dore (R.E. Kay, drawn in 1969)

a bridge over the Trenant brook, but the brook has been diverted slightly at this point and the feature no longer serves this purpose.

The GVSG's survey in 2000 showed the remains of the Trenant/Trench Royal weir and sluices that survived at that time and can be seen in Figure 9.25. These stones have now been replaced by a concrete ford for the bridleway which crosses at this point. The Trench Royal still carries water south from this point to the junction with the Shegear brook (see below), south of Poston Court Farm.

Fig. 9.25 Three sandstone slabs at site of blocking weir and overspill channel at the junction of Trenant brook and Trench Royal

Weir and site of sluice gate south of Poston Court Farm

The weir below Poston Court Farm at the junction of the former course of the Shegear brook, the Trench Royal and the lower Shegear brook was rather better preserved, but with some modifications (Fig. 9.24 b). The weir across the Trench Royal was made of concrete and therefore may be a replacement for an earlier stone and wooden structure, but there is no firm evidence for this. Fig. 9.26 below shows the remains of the weir across the Trench Royal today and shows the level of water retained in the Trench in early spring.

Fig. 9.26 Junction of Trench Royal and Shegear brook and site of sluice gate for topping trench

Kay also identified rubble-built retaining walls of laminated sandstone slabs on the west side of the Trench Royal, which varied in width from 0.7m to 1.4m near the point where it made an obtuse angle. In places it remained at a height of 1.5m above the bed of the Trench and

Fig 9.27 (a: 1960s) and (b: 2006) Sluice gate on Shegear brook at junction with Trench Royal

Fig. 9.28 Site of excavations (2015) to establish course of Shegear brook
(a) state of the sluice prior to restoration
(b) exposed paved stone base to ford
(c) the restored sluice with the brook flowing once again after heavy rain in late 2015

appeared to be of original construction. He documented this feature with a photograph taken in the late 1960s[12] (Fig. 9.27 a), which clearly shows the sluice gate opening for the Shegear brook to join the Trench Royal at this point. Since this time, the feature has been eroded by winter storms and the brook has been diverted (Figs 9.27 b & 9.28 a).

The area immediately to the west of the sluice was excavated in 2015 by the Countryside Restoration Trust to establish the original course of the Shegear brook, in the course of which a significant ford was identified. Restoration work is now complete and the Shegear brook flows again through the rebuilt sluice or 'lunky' (Fig 9.28(c)).

Fig. 9.29 Sluice for 'Topping' or 'Braving' Trench where it enters the Shegear Brook at its junction with Trench Royal (see page 44).

Below the present weir there were also vestiges of a kind of basin on the Trench Royal and on the east side a series of fragmented walls with broken foundations giving indications of a two- or three-channelled sluice at this point. The slot of the timber sluice remained in the wall of the more northerly opening (Fig. 9.29), now covered in undergrowth. This would have diverted water into a channel, traces of which remain, which runs parallel to the Trench Royal – possibly what Rowland referred to as a 'Topping or Braving Trench' (see Chapter 4).

Weirs and sluices on the lower Slough brook

Kay[13] also identified the remains of two important weirs and sluices in the lower Slough brook which he described as the 'upper' and 'lower' weirs and sluice gates (Fig. 9.30). The upper

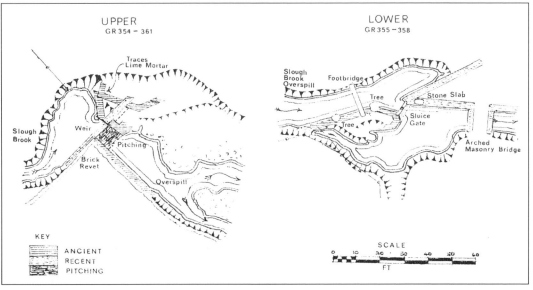

Fig. 9.30 Weirs and sluices on the lower Slough brook. (R.E. Kay, drawn in 1969)

121

weir was constructed to divert the Slough brook to run in a more southerly course, eventually to join the river Dore south of Chanstone Court Farm. The channel from this point on seems to be of artificial construction. The weir was relatively well preserved and showed works from many different periods and uses both stone and brick. The weir is of concrete and more recent construction, and there are footings for a small building on the east of the structure, but without a considerable fall in water level this could not be a mill. Since that time the feature has been significantly eroded.

The lower weir is a little downstream of the upper weir, at the junction of a channel from the Whitehouse 'port'. It seems to effect a transfer in the levels of the diverted course of the Slough brook, but has been badly eroded and the pool is now described as a 'sheepwash' (see also Fig. 9.15).

Mill Leat – Peterchurch to Poston Mill

A fourth major feature occurs where the mill leat extends for over 900m from the river Dore just south of Peterchurch to Poston Mill (No.5 on Map 9.1). The aerial photograph (Fig. 9.31) looking south-east shows the mill leat in a slight curve from the sharp curve of the river Dore, now marked by trees; an overflow channel once flowed in the dry, snake-like curved trench, linking the leat to the river in the middle of the picture. The main weir diverting the Dore (raising water levels by 3.7m) was located at the junction of the large bend in the river where it meets the leat, and a stone wall formed part of an overflow structure diverting water back to the Dore to stop the head of water getting too high at the mill.

The LIDAR tile (Fig. 9.3) also shows the weir diverting water to the mill leat leading to Poston Mill ('a' in Fig. 9.31) and second weir and the faint snake-like return channel to the river Dore to control water levels on the mill leat at Poston ('b' in Fig. 9.31). It is possible that a

Fig. 9.31 Aerial view of the origin of the Poston Court Mill leat: (a) the return channel (b) the flood plain of the river Dore. The winding line of trees indicates the course of the river.

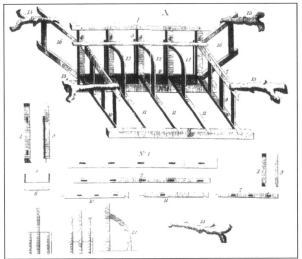

Fig. 9.32 Weir and sluice gates found in Boswell's 'Treatise on Watering Meadows' 1779

Fig, 9.33 Remnants of weir and sluice gates on river Dore – Poston Mill Leat – wooden structure with joints of mortise and tenon (a) and dovetails (b)

weir with sluice gates similar to those in Fig. 9.32 may have been situated at the head of the Poston Mill Race.

The remains of a wooden structure, similar to that shown by Boswell (Fig. 9.32) can be found today in the river Dore when it is very low and dry, with joints of mortise and tenon and dovetails (Fig 9.33).

Flood Control and Sustainable Land Use Today

In Rowland's scheme, weirs and sluices were used to spread water over carefully levelled fields, where terraces and low earth banks helped to distribute the water evenly over the land and prevent it from draining back into the river too quickly. This flooding of level ground was an early form of bedwork. The valley sides were irrigated as well, by means of channels which carried water along the contour from brooks and springs and allowed it to overflow down sloping fields. This irrigation of hillsides or catchwork is also referred to as 'contour watermeadows'. Making use of catchwork as well as of bedwork, Rowland's waterworks combine to form a hybrid system of water management which can be used for flood control, increasing fertility through silt deposition, and increasing soil temperatures to bring forward spring grasses. The irrigation regime can also be used in summer to reduce the impact of dry periods.

The development of modern water management systems in the Golden Valley could enhance more sustainable farming practices in a period of greater climate instability and extreme weather events. It could have particular value for flood management, increasing biodiversity, irrigation, and reduced run-off

Fig. 9.34 The dry riverbed of the Dore at Peterchurch in the summer of 2011

of topsoil, and modulate the impacts of extreme weather events through appropriate water management principles.

Flow data and rainfall variations for the river Dore show that in recent years the flow data has been subject to significant seasonal and annual variability in line with low and high rainfall periods. This was particularly marked between 2011 and 2012 when the high summer rainfall of 2012 contrasted markedly with the low rainfall of the previous year (Fig 9.34) compared to the more usual seasonal variation. The development of a water management system could have many benefits in smoothing these variable run-off patterns and provide flood control and irrigation for water-meadows in periods of excessive rainfall or drought.

Rowland's *water-workes* represent an amazing multi-functional water management system, regardless of whether Rowland was the innovator, or someone with the vision to implement a practical scheme. Sufficient to say that Rowland was an extraordinary country gentleman who showed understanding, ingenuity and engineering skill in exploiting the principles of hydrology and topography to enhance the productivity of the land on his estate.

10   AN APPRECIATION OF THE LIFE AND ACHIEVEMENTS OF ROWLAND VAUGHAN

In accordance with custom, Rowland as a second son had to make his own way in life. His ancestors had benefited from their support of the Tudor monarchs and as a young man with such family connections he served in the royal court of Queen Elizabeth, entered the army and on returning home married his cousin, Elizabeth Vaughan, who had inherited the manor and park of Newcourt in the Golden Valley of west Herefordshire, only a few miles from his own home. He would live there for nearly 30 years.

Few members of the minor gentry of that period in a place so remote would leave such a vivid trail of their life. He personally has supplied much of the material for this study of his achievements and, it must be admitted, his failings. His story emerges from three main sources – firstly *His Booke*, secondly the evidence arising from at least 16 informative lawsuits and thirdly the fading landmarks spread along the local landscape indicating the irrigation waterworks for which he became best known.

Only a few original copies of *His Booke* are known to survive but in 1897 a new edition was published by Ellen Beatrice Wood, who lived at Molewood near Hertford. This opened interest in Rowland's work, both in Herefordshire and later amongst agricultural historians. The research and articles were concentrated upon Rowland's waterworks but from the mid-20th century academic agricultural historians spread the field wider across southern England. Now in 2015 Historic England is embarking on a nationwide survey.

It might be thought that the trail in the Golden Valley has been well trodden. However, not only has the ground been re-examined meticulously by inhabitants of the Golden Valley familiar with its roads and paths, streams and springs, lying pools and frosted hollows, but a wider range of research can now be based on digital search material not even available until a few years ago and archives not previously scoured. From this array of evidence, new and old, we do not have to rely on Rowland's self-admittedly exaggerated anecdotes. Instead, we can directly hear his plaintiff appeals, hold his flamboyant signatures in the hand and trace his numerous business dealings.

We can meet Rowland, the man of action, ambitious, self-important and unafraid to press forward his own views, adventurous but prone to make rash decisions. Moreover, we also witness the difficulties that these brought upon him and the disasters which led to his increasing belligerence and troubles. Conversely, we also find that shortcomings were balanced by the devotion of his three successive wives and other womenfolk.

Among the last was his young niece Joan Winston, living in Standish, Gloucestershire with a hostile step-mother. Rowland took her into his own home but about 1605 ran into trouble in the Court of Wards over his guardianship. The case ran for ten years and he was right to blame it for later problems. It may seem a mere sideline but it was crucial. He not only neglected, and then had to restore, the waterworks built in his absence whilst he attended the London law courts but he built up heavy debts to city moneylenders to add to those arising from his land purchases. He would never break clear of them to his dying day.

It should be kept in mind that when *His Booke* was published in 1610 he was already 52 years old, a good age for the period. He had not only launched his experimental irrigation scheme at Bacton, he had also established the iron forge at Peterchurch, bought and disposed of property within a radius of ten or more miles of Bacton, was responsible as patron for the oversight of three or four of the local churches and had given serious thought to solutions for local poverty. In addition he was spending more time in London than at home. All were enough to fill his time – but at this stage the waterworks remained his prime interest.

He claimed that he had never seen waterworks such as those that he started on the river Dore at Bacton soon after his first marriage in 1582. Despite his habit of exaggeration there is no reason to doubt his word. It would have been too easy to prove him wrong and people ranging from farmers in the Golden Valley to the Lord Chief Justice in London thought it a crazy idea. For centuries people had been familiar with the working of watermills and their leats and some medieval Cistercian monasteries had deployed irrigation schemes. In the 16th century a few agricultural writers recommended the feeding of pastures from waste domestic waters and overflowing floods. Although there is no direct mention of a monastic irrigation scheme, either in Dore Abbey's archives or from a legal inquiry in Rowland's time concerning mills at Bacton, we have seen evidence, particularly from LIDAR, for water-meadow management to the south of the abbey. A similar practice began at about the same time in the chalklands of Dorset and Wiltshire, where by coincidence Rowland's patron, the 3rd earl of Pembroke had his seat at Wilton, but no connection between the landowners has been established.

If Rowland had no previous knowledge of other waterworks, whether ancient or contemporary, we must look elsewhere to find his incentive to explore water and its powers. This was the man who, writing about his prospective first marriage, was more attracted by the overshot watermill on her estate than her virtues as a bride. He had grown up on the banks of the river Wye, a river that annually flooded the nearby meadows. Settled at Bacton, he was attracted by the power of water in other ways, for conveying his timber downstream, driving a sawmill, working the Peterchurch forge, and hauling goods upstream in preference to dragging them over Herefordshire's notorious highways. Water could turn the wheels in the kitchen and serve other domestic purposes. In the drawing of his mythical Commonwealth (Fig. 5.3, page 61) streams run past, through or beneath the principal buildings.

His waterworks at Bacton were probably started under his oversight from about 1590 or a little sooner. The doubt is caused by the erratic dating in *His Booke* written to describe his aims and explain his plan which he appears to have started in 1604. It is not an easy book to follow. Rowland himself admitted that he had embellished the text to attract attention, so the reader should not expect it to be precisely accurate. By then he could boast of success for the irrigation and the flooding to the extent that he could claim that after a few years the costs were met by the improvement of the grazing and increased number of beasts that could be pastured. This, of course, was his intention – to improve the value of the meadows and so enrich the estate – and this was a high point. The waterworks were sufficiently well advanced for him to show them off proudly to other landowners and to contemplate advertising his success by publication.

The earliest known meadow drownings in Dorset, inarguably recorded in manorial documents, were being made between 1605 and 1610. In the past authors credited Rowland alone with the invention of drowning on the evidence of the publication of *His Booke* in 1610. Clearly the early irrigations in Wessex now make this uncertain and other early schemes may be revealed in the new nationwide research commissioned by Historic England. However, from our researches we are satisfied that he was among the first landowners to create a full working system of irrigation in England and that *His Booke* is the first publication devoted to a detailed description of the methods and benefits of drowning.

This leads to the question of how effective was Rowland's dissemination of his achievement. Clearly he was ready to talk about it to anyone who would listen. In the Golden Valley his works were well known, if not always approved of, and the early drowning of meadows in other parts of Herefordshire suggests that other local landowners followed his example. Ellen Beatrice Wood, when she reprinted Rowland's book in 1897, could find only four copies of the original version printed by George Eld, the well-known London printer-publisher who had printed the first edition of Shakespeare's *Sonnets* the previous year. From the note at the end of *His Booke* we gather that copies were printed for Rowland himself to sell. A passing reference to *His Booke* in John Smyth (d.1641), *Lives of the Berkeleys,* shows that Rowland was known in Gloucestershire and a copy seen by Ellen Beatrice Wood had been in the hands of an owner in west Brecon. They had therefore become widely scattered. Whether by sale, gift or word of mouth, news of the benefits of drowning spread rapidly within Rowland's lifetime.

It is more difficult to determine how and for how long the completed waterworks were maintained. In the last 17 years of his life amid the many lawsuits relating to his debts and numerous battles with the members of his family and neighbours, there is no mention of the waterworks or their value. In giving evidence about his life, he never speaks of the scheme for which he is now best known. The closest members of his family, in their continuing efforts to settle his debts or transfer his property to themselves, also ignored what Rowland had considered his prime investment. Rowland himself also turned his attention to his more pressing troubles in his attempts to hold on to his home at Whitehouse. Later, among the archives of the Whitehouse estate at the end of the 18th century there are two fleeting references in tenancy agreements to the maintenance of the drains, floodgates and weirs on the estate and as late as 1878, when the Poston estate was put up for sale, mention was made of its water-meadows 'abundantly irrigated by the River Dore and its tributaries'.[1]

Over time Rowland's pioneering works for the whole valley were becoming reduced by silt, storm and neglect, leaving only the Trench Royal and its links with the river Dore and the streams flowing down from the brooks to the west, and the few remains of their weirs and sluices. The Golden Valley still bears relics of Rowland's 400-year-old waterworks. Ellen Beatrice Wood had overlooked them on her brief visits because she had concentrated on the meadows of Newcourt, not Whitehouse. According to information handed down by A.S. Wood (who inherited Whitehouse but was not related to Ellen Beatrice Wood), parts of the system were in use at the turn of the 19th century. By 1943, when his daughter Penelope wrote an undergraduate essay on the subject, it was out of use and since then its landmarks have been steadily disappearing. Selective surveys in 1973, 1983 and 2004 have filled some gaps. The present study by the GVSG, using the latest research aids and a wide use of archives from The National Archives, the National Library of Wales, the Herefordshire Archives and Records Centre and other sources has aimed to bring our knowledge of Rowland and his waterworks up to date.

We cannot do better than repeat Rowland Vaughan's closing words from *His Booke*[2] addressed to his patron William, Lord Herbert, earl of Pembroke:

> Howsoever, as this Worke, now finished, is published for thy profit, and exprest in such manner as I thought would yeeld thee most pleasure: so thou wilt accept it kindly, and thereby give me cause to be ever studious of thy benefit.

Our own view is that Rowland's methods of water regulation may have relevance for farming practices today as we experience increasing instability in rainfall patterns and extremes of drought or flood.

THE CONCLUSION[3]

Thus runnes our Water-workes unto this end,
That all that worke by them, by them may play:
For, if they Mossy-grounds by them amend,
For paines and pleasures (then) they'l freely pay.
This WORKE consists not (like some idle Tracts)
In shew alone, or Speculation:
No; this is practicall, faire shewes in Acts,
To make the poor'st, the richest Nation.
Then, chiefly amy'd I not ar publick-good,
I would not thus divulge my private skill:
But bee'ng free-borne, my Natur's like my Blood;
Which would do good to all, and no man ill:
Then, All (I hope) or of that All, the best
Will wish me well: as for the rest, I rest.
Theirs as they give me cause,[4]

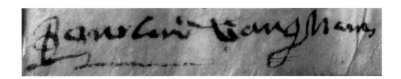

FINIS

129

Notes and References

Chapter 1 Introduction

1. Rowland Vaughan, Esq., *Most Approved and Long experienced Water Workes,* 1610, republished and prefaced by Ellen Beatrice Wood, ed., as *Rowland Vaughan, his Booke: Published 1610,* John Hodges, London, 1897. Referred to hereafter as *His Booke.* All page references are to the 1897 edition.
2. *His Booke,* p.36.
3. Brian Smith, 'The Gilden Vale', in *Turnastone: Stability and change in the Herefordshire countryside 1800-2000,* 2010, p.7.
4. John & Sheila Rowlands, *The Surnames of Wales,* 1996, pp.157-8.
5. M.A. Faraday, ed., *Herefordshire taxes in the reign of Henry VIII,* 2005.
6. *His Booke,* p.82.
7. *His Booke,* p.31.
8. M.A. Faraday, ed., *Herefordshire Militia Assessments of 1663,* 1972, p.117.
9. This is the term used by Rowland to refer to his workers or artisans.
10. *His Booke,* p.53.
11. *His Booke,* p.43.
12. R.S. Gavin Robinson, 'Rowland Vaughan and his Water-Works', *Trans WNFC,* 1936, pp.35-38.
13. Timothy J.R. Wood and Arthur Seward Wood, *A short history of Whitehouse, Vowchurch, Herefordshire and its owners,* privately printed, 2000.

Chapter 2 The Vaughan Family

1. Francis Smalman (d.1633) and his wife Susan had a daughter Jane, a distant relative to Rowland through her marriage to Rowland Howorth, son of Epiphan Howorth.
2. Presumably Sir Roger descended from a younger son who took the Welsh name Fychan/Vaughan.
3. David Whitehead, *A Survey of Historic Parks & Gardens in Herefordshire,* 2001, p.47, quoting a 12th-century charter of Ralph de Baskerville.
4. Ellen Beatrice Wood, ed., republished 1897. For full citation see chapter 1.
5. John Guy, *Tudor England,* 1988, p.417. 'Bible' English evolved through the widespread use of William Tyndale's translation of *The New Testament* and Thomas Cranmer's *Book of Common Prayer.* It can be found in the vernacular English of the law courts, in Puritan bibles and even in popular ballads.
6. *His Booke,* p.150.
7. Alan Brooks & Nikolaus Pevsner, *The buildings of England, Herefordshire,* 2012, p.515.
8. We are grateful to David Whitehead for this research. See Ashmead-Price, *Moccas Court: Parkland Plan,* 2013, pp.5-33, copy in HARC.
9. David Whitehead, *op.cit.,* 2001, p.271.
10. Brian Smith, *Herefordshire Maps 1577 to 1800,* 2004: Saxton was selective in including deer parks. Certainly abandoned, or non-maintained ones were omitted.
11. *His Booke,* pp.66-7.
12. Hatfield MS Cal. Vol.7, p.180.
13. Milo (Mylo) was also known as Myles ap Harry. His brother Symond/Simon anglicised his own name to Parry. As a result of this Symond named his brother as Myles Parry in his will of 1573.
14. As the male line did not continue, Parry descendants usually derive from their cousins the Parrys of Poston. Theophilus Jones, *The History of Brecknockshire,* pp.442-3, 1805; HARC B56/2.

15. John Guy, *op.cit.*, 1988, p.373. By Henry VIII's reign wardships had become a valuable source of income for the Crown.

16. A letter to the Lord Keeper: '...*where we have received like comendacions from the said Earl* [Pembroke] *in the behalf of Charles Bridges of Wiltshire esquire, to supplie the office of Lieutenancie in stead of Roger Bodenham of Rotherns* [Rotherwas] *esquire, in the countie of Hereford...and that Mr Walter* [Watkyn] *Vaughan, being verie aged and unapt to travel, may be verie wel supplied by his sonne and heir, Henry Vaughan, in the Deputy Lieutenancie of the countie of Brecon.*' Acts of the Privy Council 31 May 1593.

17. http://historyofparliamentonline.org/volume/1558-1603/member/vaughan-watkin [accessed April 2015].

18. *Calendar of State Papers Elizabeth vol.3, 1584.*

19. Family mattered a great deal to Watkyn Vaughan for in 1556 he had stood bail for Katherine Vaughan of Pentwyn who was accused of being an accessory to felony and murder.

20. In Tudor society the eldest son would inherit everything by primogeniture. Second or later sons could be disadvantaged. Their inheritance often depended on specific bequests in their father's will. A godchild was often named after the most prestigious godparent who in turn was expected to help the child advance in life.

21. R. Haslam, The buildings of Wales, Powys, 1992, p.372; C.J. Robinson, A history of the castles of Herefordshire and their lords, 1869, pp.21-24.

22. R.E. Richardson, *Mistress Blanche, Queen Elizabeth I's Confidante*, 2007, p.156.

23. J. Nichols, The Progresses and Public Processions of Queen Elizabeth, 1823.

24. TNA, STAC/V8/27. The unequal partition of the Parry estates may have been the reason for the agreement for paying a buck and doe from Newcourt Park to Watkyn and Joan. C6/191/101.

25. T. Brook, *Mr Selden's map of China*, 2013, p.23.

26. Hatfield MS Cal. Vol.7, p.180.

27. *His Booke,* p.81.

28. State Papers Domestic, Acts of the Privy Council.

29. *His Booke,* pp.81-2.

30. *Ibid.*, p.57.

31. Blanche had bequeathed £100 to Elizabeth in her first, nuncupative will, but Elizabeth by now was dead.

32. *His Booke,* p.82.

33. R.E. Richardson, *op.cit.*, 2007, pp.91-97.

34. In 1566 Sir Roger Vaughan had conveyed estates including Newcourt and Bacton to Henry Lord Herbert, Edward Herbert and John Vaughan of Escrick (which had been his wife's inheritance). This John Vaughan was Blanche Parry's nephew, son of her and Milo ap Harry's sister, in trust for himself, Elizabeth (widow of Rowland Vaughan of Porthaml) and her children.

35. *His Booke,* p.67.

36. Both sisters were then minors. TNA, STAC/V8/27.

37. A reasonable assumption due to the evidence that the Winston children, who were as wild as hawks, tried to run away back to Joan, their grandmother in Bredwardine when their new step-mother tried to instil a little discipline into their young lives. The oldest Winston boy, Henry, when he grew up asked to be buried in Bredwardine church rather than at Standish, which also argues for the Vaughans giving them pleasant childhood memories!

38. TNA, PROB11/61 Will of Margaret Dane. Katherine Vaughan, then Blanche Parry's waiting woman, was to have a cup worth £20 on the day of her marriage to Robert Knollys.

39. *His Booke,* p.82.

40. *Ibid,* p.82.

41. NLW, Tredegar 72/3, Arbitration 23 November 1583 records William as deceased.

42. HARC, Hereford Diocesan Probates - First Series (1540-1600): Elizabeth Whitney of Bacton (New Court) 1583, 44/3/43.

43. Currency conversion 1570/2005, www.nationalarchives.gov.uk/currency. It is notoriously difficult to make price comparisons over such a long period and all such figures should be treated warily. In Rowland Vaughan's lifetime prices rose steeply.

44. TNA, STAC5/P15/4.

45. TNA, C2/Eliz/G15/26; NLW Powis12659.

46. TNA, NLW, Tredegar 72/3, 137/94, Penpont Supp 764.

47. TNA, STAC5/P15/4.

48. R.E. Richardson, *op.cit.*, 2007, pp.115-121.

49. TNA, STAC5/V8/27. This date is taken from a lawsuit eight years after the event.

50. A drawing of Newcourt *c*.1814 shows a symmetrically-faced and crenelated mansion of late 17th- or 18th-century appearance; Ruth E. Richardson, *Mistress Blanche, Queen Elizabeth's Confidante*, 2007, p.30, quoting Hereford City Library, Pilley Collection. It does not resemble the principal house in Vaughan's sketch (Fig.4.3) of his imaginary Commonwealth in *His Booke* published in 1610 shortly before he left Newcourt.

51. *His Booke, e.g.* pp.34-35.

52. Bacton tithe map, 1842 & apportion-ment 1839, and St. Margaret's tithe map 1844 & apportionment 1846, originals in Herefordshire Record Office; Ruth E. Richardson, ed., *The Herefordshire Field-Name Survey 1986-1993*; http://htt.herefordshire.gov.uk/1384.aspx [accessed May 2015].

53. Gwent Record Office MAN/A/ 151/0024 A 1624 survey of the manor of Ewyas Lacy section referring to the location of land granted to Robert Hopton and his wife Elizabeth.

54. The present road at Newton is in the original park boundary ditch. Other traces of the bank and ditch can still be seen and can be compared to the 1624 survey.

55. TNA, STAC5/V8/27. The date of 1611 given by A.S. Wood, *A short history of Whitehouse and its owners*, (privately printed 1954, revised by T.J.R. Wood, 2000) is incorrect and is a misreading of the wording in a Chancery case of 1612, TNA, C2/Jas1/C4/7. Wood also mentions their son John (correct) but also, incorrectly, a daughter Jane who married Stephen Parry of Morehampton. In fact Stephen and Jane were of an earlier generation.

56. TNA, C2/JasI/C4/7: a 1612 case of Carwardyne v Vaughan concerning land at Newcourt, refers to Rowland Vaughan of Whitehouse esq. and Elizabeth his late wife who '*had issue John (son and heir) and divers other issue.*' The only record of '*William Vaughan son of Rowland Vaughan esq.*' appears in 1599 when he was appointed co-executor of the will of Robert Vaughan of Vowchurch.

57. Humfry Howorth's evidence E112/302/17; Anne Jones was also an heiress to an estate.

58. *His Booke,* p.83.

Chapter 3 The Suitability of 'The Gilden Vale' for a System of Waterworks

1. Rosamund Skelton, *The Golden Valley Archaeological Survey,* unpublished Report for the Manpower Services Commission (MSC), 1982-83, Historic Environment Record (HER), HARC.

2. Sheila Harvey & Brian Smith, 'Cothill Farm', in *Turnastone: Stability and change in the Herefordshire countryside 1800-2000*, 2010, p.81.

3. Carolina Lane, 'The Development of Pastures and Meadows during the Sixteenth and Seventeenth Centuries,' *Agricultural History Review* 28(1), 1980, pp.18–30.

4. Carolina Lane, *ibid.*

5. Master Fitzherbert, *The Boke of Husbandry,* 1523, and *The Boke of Surveyeng*, 1523.

6. John Norden, *The Surveyor's Dialogue*, 1610.

7. E. Kerridge, *op. cit.,* 1967.

8. Hadrian Cook, Kathy Stearn & Tom Williamson, 'The origins of water-meadows in England', *AgHR* 51(2), 2003, pp.155-62.

9. Cook *et al., ibid.*

10. R.A. Donkin, *The Cistercians: studies in the geography of medieval England and Wales,* 1978.

11. Historic England, Heritage Gateway, HER number (PRN) 03390 *Water Meadows W of Buildwas Abbey*, 1997. http://www.heritage-gateway.org.uk/Gateway/Results_Single.aspx?uid=MSA2186&resourceID=1015 [accessed July 2015].

12. *His Booke*, p.36.

13. William Camden, *Britannia*, first published in Latin in 1586; English in 1610 and revised 1722.

14. G. Charnock, *South West Herefordshire Post Glacial Landscape & Settlement Features,* Talk to Woolhope Club, Ewyas Lacy Study Group Documents, 2001. http://www.ewyaslacy.

org.uk/-/Postglacial-Landscape-of-SW-Herefordshire/to-10-000-BC/gc_gdv_3000 [accessed June 2015].

15. C.P. Burnham 'The Soils of Herefordshire', in *Soil Survey of Great Britain*, Agricultural Research Council, 1964 (cited by Golden Valley Archaeological Survey, HER, 1983-4).

16. Herefordshire Council, *Landscape Character Assessment (LCA) and SPG*, 2004 (updated 2009).

17. E.L Jones 'Agricultural Conditions and Agricultural Changes in Herefordshire 1660-1815' *Trans WNFC* 37, 1961, pp.32-55.

18. R. Shoesmith & Ruth E. Richardson, eds., *A definitive history of Dore Abbey*, 1997, p.30.

Chapter 4 Cistercian waterworks at Dore Abbey and later developments by Rowland at Bacton

1. R. Shoesmith & R. Richardson, *A definitive history of Dore Abbey*, 1997.

2. The term LIDAR was created from a fusion of the words 'light' and 'radar'. It is a remote sensing technology for illuminating a target with a laser and analysing the reflected light (Wikipedia). In this study the LIDAR images are produced using laser imaging technology set to record the sub-surface features at different depths. These point records are then transformed to create LIDAR tile surfaces which define the landform features below the current surface.

3. H. Cook, K. Stearn & T. Williamson, *op. cit.*, 2003.

4. Hadrian Cook, 'The Hydrology, Soils and Geology of the Wessex Water Meadows', in *Water Meadows History, Ecology and Conservation*', eds. Hadrian Cook and Tom Williamson, Ch. 8, 2007.

5. *His Booke*, p.94.

6. Hadrian Cook, *op.cit.*

7. E. Kerridge, 'Floating the Watermeadows', *The Agricultural Revolution*, 1967, pp.251-67.

8. 1832 Ordnance Survey Map sheet 161 – Cassini Edition.

9. *His Booke*, p.121.

10. *His Booke*, p.110 (paraphrased).

11. *His Booke*, p.120.

12. *His Booke*, pp.108-9 (paraphrased).

13. *His Booke*, p.110.

14. *His Booke*, pp.131-2 (paraphrased).

15. TNA, STACS/V8/27.

16. He was also the last steward of Dore abbey.

17. Bacton tithe map 1842 & apportionment 1839. Field 58 is 'Lower Monk homs'; Field 57 has no recorded name but was almost certainly 'Upper Monk homs' (see Map 4.4, bottom right). Ordnance Survey grid reference SO377324.

18. *His Booke*, pp.83-84.

19. HARC, F35/RC/HII/9-17 and AL40/1882.

20. HARC, BH59/99 and F94/II/9.

21. TNA, C115/34.

22. HARC, F37/7.

23. HARC, AW28/25/12.

Chapter 5 The Enterprising Squire

1. For example, Ellen Beatrice Wood when editing *His Booke*, and A.S. Wood, 'Comments upon the Herefordshire environment in the 17th and 18th centuries', *Trans WNFC*, vol.36, pt.2, 1959, pp.202-204.

2. Hereford City Library typescript, C.A. Bradford, *Rowland Vaughan an unknown Elizabethan*, quoting TNA, SP12, vol.211, No.81; this study was subsequently published by E.T. Heron & Co., 1937.

3. *His Booke*, p.71.

4. TNA, STAC8/288/2; N. MacGregor, *Shakespeare's restless world*, 2012, pp.64, 107.

5. J.C. Eisel, 'Aspects of the Wye navigation', *Trans WNFC*, vol.60, 2012, pp.25-27; H. Hurley, *Herefordshire's river trade*, 2013, pp.3-6.

6. J. van Laun, '17th-century ironworking in south-west Herefordshire', *Historical Metallurgy Journal*, vol.13, no.2, 1979, p.58.

7. *His Booke*, p.152.

8. *Victoria County History of Gloucestershire*, vol.5, Forest of Dean, *passim*.

9. K. Wrighton, *English society 1580-1680*, 1982, pp.52-54.

10. TNA, C2/Eliz/P2/56.

11. J. van Laun, *op. cit.*, pp. 55-68; English Heritage, National Monuments Record, *Record Card, Herefordshire, Peterchurch*, Monument 6, 1931; HARC, BD20/21/1, Inett Homes Collection.

12. C.A. Bradford, *Blanche Parry, Queen Elizabeth's Gentlewoman,* 1935, pp.21-22.

13. Historical Manuscripts Commission, *Calendar of the Manuscripts of the Marquis of Salisbury,* vol.7, 1899, p.180.

14. HARC, F37/8 and 10.

15. W.E. Tate, *The parish chest,* 1946, p.190.

16. *His Booke,* p.31.

17. Ellen Beatrice Wood and other writers have misread his wording and taken Vaughan's vision as a fact. See J.C. Davis, *Utopia and the ideal society; a study of English Utopian writing 1516-1700,* 1981, pp.308-313.

18. *His Booke,* pp.33-35, 68.

19. *Ibid.* pp.72-74.

20. *Ibid.* pp.76-77.

21. *Ibid.* p.64.

22. Some sources (notably R. *Mathias, Whitsun Riot. An account of a commotion amongst Catholics in Herefordshire and Monmouthshire in 1605,* 1963, p.42) have confused Griffith Jones with Griffin ap Powell, who also died in 1578, with a daughter named Anne, recorded in the contemporary Mylborne family pedigree in J.A. Bradney, ed., *Llyfr Baglan 1600-1607 by John Williams,* 1910, p.44. We have accepted the version recorded by the Howorth family and descendants, including Humfrey Howorth of Whitehouse in 1655 (E112/302/17 *King's Remembrancer Bills and Answers Commonwealth, Herefordshire*) who stated '*Rowland Vaughan about 60 years ago married Anne daughter of Griffith Jones and Jane his wife, the said Anne being an inheritrix of the Whitehouse and a parcel of wood (200a) called Whitehouse Wood and all other lands belonging, and the said Rowland Vaughan was seised of the Whitehouse in right of Anne his wife*'; and subsequently A.S. Wood in *A short history of Whitehouse, Vowchurch, Herefordshire and its owners* (privately printed 1954, revised T.J.R. Wood, 2000). Fresh research has been made of entries in the *Welsh Medieval Databases of Family Search, Community Trees* for Anne Jones 1234272, Jane Parry 1233599, Gruffedd Jones 1233530 and 1233531 (2008). See also 'Howorth of Whitehouse', *Visitation of Herefordshire 1634,* Harleian Society NS15,

2002, p.10, (Blanch Jones); wills of Symond Parry [mis-indexed as 'Aprame'] 1573, PCC Peter PROB11/55/313; Griffith Jones of Llowes 1578, PCC Langley PROB11/60/381. The latter will, proved 28 June 1578, refers to Whitehouse and his arrangement *c.*1569 to put his estates in trust to Sir James Whitney for Jane, base child of Margaret Hyggins.

23. TNA, C2/Eliz/U2/44.

24. This is the only reference found to Rowland's second son William. He was presumably representing the family while his father was in London and John in Oxford.

25. TNA, C3/293/94.

26. TNA, C3/387/40 (1624). Epiphan Howorth's claim on Whitehouse partially rested upon a conveyance from Richard Vaughan as son and heir of Rowland Vaughan, which legally could only have been through his mother Anne. See also E112/302/17 *op.cit.,* 1655.

27. Joseph Foster, ed., *Alumni Oxoniensis 1500 – 1714,* 1891, p.1536.

Chapter 6 Drowning the Valley: the northern section from Peterchurch to Turnastone

1. George Boswell, *Treatise on Watering Meadows,* 1779.

2. This map © Cassini Publishing Ltd is reproduced here by the kind permission of the publishers. Many other historical maps at a range of scales and periods are available from www.cassinimaps.com.

3. See notes to Chapter 4 for a brief explanation of LIDAR imaging.

4. GVSG is grateful to David Lovelace for his skilled generation of the LIDAR images and maps, and for his collaboration in their interpretation.

5. Paraphrased from *His Booke,* pp.92-4.

6. R.C. Ward & M. Robinson, *Principles of Hydrology,* 1990, p.241.

7. Paraphrased from *His Booke,* pp.87-8.

8. Boswell, *op.cit.,* 1779.

Chapter 7 Rowland Vaughan, the Church and Family Life

1. *His Booke*, p.43.
2. J. Childs, *God's traitors. Terror and faith in Elizabethan England,* 2014, pp.291, 354.
3. R. *Mathias, Whitsun Riot. An account of a commotion amongst Catholics in Herefordshire and Monmouthshire in 1605,* 1963, pp.122-3, 131.
4. Mark Nicholls, 'Watson, William (1559?–1603)', *Oxford Dictionary of National Biography*, online edn, 2008 [accessed 27 Feb 2015].
5. The mob is said to have gathered at 5.30 in the morning. On 21 May the sun would have risen about 4 a.m., GMT.
6. Mathias, *op.cit.* 1963, pp.49-51; Wikipedia (http://en.wikipedia.org/wiki/Cwm,_Llanrothal [accessed Jan 2015]). We also thank Mrs Mary Walsh for allowing us to visit The Cwm.
7. HARC, HD4.
8. *His Booke*, p.41.
9. *His Booke*, p.41.
10. *Ibid.* pp.38-41.
11. HARC, HD4/1/156-161, HD4/2/17, HD5/1/3, 7-12.
12. HARC, HD5/1/7.
13. *His Booke*, pp.43-44, 40.
14. *Ibid.* pp.40, 44, 67-68. Vowchurch and Turnastone officially came together in 1936; Peterchurch and Dorstone were added in 1957; nevertheless all remain as separate parishes with a shared incumbent. A further reorganisation in 2000 created a new benefice comprising Madley, Peterchurch, Turnastone, Tyberton and Vowchurch.
15. HARC, HD/1/165 and 168.
16. The contemporary but crude board hung by the screen at Vowchurch contains a motto (*Vive ut postea vivas*), fairly common at the time, and used elsewhere as a signatory by John Abel, the Herefordshire master carpenter (1578/9-1675). The antiquary Richard Gough (1735-1809) was the first to attribute the roof and screen to Abel, as cautiously does D. Whitehead in the *Oxford Dictionary of National Biography*, 2004 and Alan Brooks and Nikolaus Pevsner, *The buildings of England, Herefordshire*, 2012,

p.635. But the Vowchurch carpentry is not of Abel's standard and his earliest recorded works date only from 1625. As a younger man he may have started as a mill-wright, and could possibly be identified as John the joiner, referred to by Rowland in *His Booke,* pp.87-88. A second board by the Vowchurch screen records that 'Heare below ly the body of Thomas Hill ande Marget his wife, whose children made this skryne'.
17. *His Booke*, pp.89-92.
18. *Victoria County History, Gloucestershire*, vol.10, p.241; Gloucestershire Archives, D678/1; T2/1/1-39; *International Genealogical Index*; memorial in Standish church, with effigies removed to Long Burton, Dorset.
19. Wills of Lady Diones Winston, 7 April 1609 and of Henry Winston, 17 April 1614, in which he left £20 to '*his servant Rowland Vaughan*'.
20. TNA, STAC8/288/1 and 2.
21. The name is variously spelt 'Walcot' or 'Walcott' in different sources.
22. *His Booke*, p.90.
23. *His Booke.* p.130.
24. *His Booke*, pp.74-75.
25. *His Booke*, pp.48, 90.
26. *His Booke*, p.91.
27. Lincoln's Inn registers.
28. J.R. Burton, *History of the family of Walcott*, 1930; Shropshire Archives, Walcott papers.
29. *His Booke*, pp.91-92.
30. TNA, C3/387/40
31. J. Guy, *Tudor England*, 1988, p.421.
32. HARC, K11/LC3311.
33. TNA, STAC8/288/7.
34. HARC, HD4/1/171, HD4/1/172, F94/II/2.
35. TNA, STAC8/288/6.
36. TNA, STAC8/288/6; STAC8/97/1; C3/387/13.
37. HARC, F94/II/49.
38. HARC, AW28/25/11 and 12.

Chapter 8 A very Polliticke Gent'

1. *His Booke*, xxxii.
2. TNA, C3/387/13 and C3/387/40.
3. C. Bridenbaugh, *Vexed and troubled Englishmen, 1590-1642*, 1976, p.148.

136

4. *Ex inf.* D. Tong of Kingstone, builder, 16 January 2014.
5. HARC, F37/7.
6. N. MacGregor, *Shakespeare's restless world,* 2012, p.110; *The Times,* 'Saturday Review', 20 April 2013, pp.6-8.
7. TNA, C3/387/13.
8. TNA, C3/387/13.
9. TNA, STAC8/288/2.
10. HARC, K11/LC 3311.
11. HARC, AW28/25/9 and 10. M.A. Faraday, *The Herefordshire musters of 1539 and 1542,* 2012 and *Herefordshire militia assessments of 1663,* 1972, which do not record the name Morgan in Blakemere, but it does occur in Blackmoor in 1663. The Morgans of Blackmoor were related to Rowland Vaughan's family; will of Henry Winston of Standish, 17.4.1614.
12. TNA, C3/387/40 and C2/Jas I/U3/42.
13. NLW, Penpont 937 and Penpont Supp.764; TNA, E134/11/James 1/East 26; TNA, C3/387/13.
14. TNA, C3/387/40.
15. TNA, STAC8/288/2.
16. TNA, STAC8/288/8.
17. TNA, C2/JasI/H16/3.
18. TNA, C3/387/13.
19. *Ibid.*
20. TNA, C3/387/40.
21. TNA, C3/387/13 and 40; NLW, Mynde 186.
22. TNA, C115/34.
23. TNA, STAC8/288/7.
24. His will was recorded in an early probate register of Hereford diocesan wills (HARC), but despite extensive searches the will itself is among a number that have long been missing. Owing to mistaken identities both Ellen Beatrice Wood (Introduction to *His Booke*) and C.A. Bradford in *Rowland Vaughan,* pp. 8-10 have given other dates for Rowland Vaughan's death.
25. HARC, F 37/10.
26. HARC, F 37/9.
27. The Vaughan arms (*Sable a chevron between three boys heads couped at the shoulders crined Or entwined about the neck of each a serpent Proper*) are, incorrectly, displayed on the sinister side, whereas dexter are impaled the arms of the family's mythical ancestors Bleddyn ap Maenyrch (*Sable a chevron between 3 spearheads Argent*).

Chapter 9 Exploring the Relics
1. K. Stearne, 'Water meadows, Conflict, Compromise and Change', *GVSG Newsletter,* Sept.2004, p.5.
2. *Ibid.*
3. Nicky Smith, *Post medieval water systems at Turnastone Court,* English Heritage Report AI/19, 2004.
4. Rosamund Skelton, *The Golden Valley Archaeological Survey,* unpublished Report for the Manpower Services Commission (MSC), 1982-83, Historic Environment Record (HER), HARC.
5. *His Booke,* pp.124-126.
6. Nicky Smith, *op. cit.,* 2004.
7. HARC BH37/153 *Survey of the Whitehouse Estate* undated, probably 1833.
8. Rosamund Skelton, *op. cit.,* 1983.
9. G. Atwood 'A study of the Wiltshire water meadows' *Wilts.Arch.and Nat.Hist.Mag.* 58, 1964, pp.403-13.
10. Isaac Taylor, *Map of Herefordshire,* 1786, HARC LD/rs0001.
11. R.E. Kay 'Some Notes on R. Vaughan's "Waterworks" in the Golden Valley', *Trans WNFC* 41, 1974, pp.253-55.
12. BW photograph found in the papers for the Golden Valley Archaeological Survey, Skelton *op.cit.,* 1983.
13. R.E. Kay, *op.cit.,* 1974.

Chapter 10 An Appreciation of the Life and Achievements of Rowland Vaughan
1. HARC, F37/114, F37/139, and E1/5.
2. p.150.
3. *His Booke,* p.153.
4. Rowland's signature from HARC AW28/25/16-2. Photographed by Rhys Griffith.

INDEX OF PERSONAL NAMES

Women are shown under their married names with their maiden names in square brackets;
they also appear under their maiden names (if known). Peers are listed under their titles and surnames.

RV = Rowland Vaughan, subject of this book

INDEX OF PLACES

143

INDEX OF TOPICS